Happiness

Essential Mindfulness Practices

Thich Nhat Hanh

EasyRead Large

Copyright Page from the Original Book

Parallax Press
P.O. Box 7355
Berkeley, California 94707

Parallax Press is the publishing division of Unified Buddhist Church, Inc.
© 2009 by Unified Buddhist Church.
All rights reserved.
Printed in the United States of America.

Material for the practices in this book comes primarily from *How to Enjoy Your Stay in Plum Village*, *Chanting from the Heart*, *Present Moment Wonderful Moment*, and *The World We Have*, all published by Parallax Press, as well as unpublished Dharma talks by Thich Nhat Hanh.

Thank you to the United Kingdom Community of Interbeing (www.interbeing.org.uk/) for permission to reprint the Tea Ceremony.

Cover and text design by Gopa & Ted2, Inc.

Library of Congress Cataloging-in-Publication Data

Nhât Hanh, Thích.
  Happiness : essential mindfulness practices / Thich Nhat Hanh.
    p. cm.
  "Material for the practices in this book comes from How to Enjoy Your Stay in Plum Village, Chanting from the Heart, Present Moment Wonderful Moment, and The World We Have, all published by Parallax Press, and unpublished Dharma talks by Thich Nhat Hanh."
  ISBN 978-1-888375-91-6
  1. Religious life—Buddhism. I. Title.
  BQ5395.N45 2009
  294.3'4446—dc22
                                        2009013976

1 2 3 4 5 / 13 12 11 10 09

TABLE OF CONTENTS

INTRODUCTION	i
DAILY PRACTICES	
CONSCIOUS BREATHING	3
SITTING MEDITATION	13
WALKING MEDITATION	20
WAKING UP	28
THE BELL	32
TELEPHONE MEDITATION	38
BOWING	41
GATHAS	43
I HAVE ARRIVED, I AM HOME	47
TAKING REFUGE	52
THE FIVE MINDFULNESS TRAINING	54
EATING PRACTICES	
MINDFUL EATING	63
THE FIVE CONTEMPLATIONS	70
THE KITCHEN	73
TEA MEDITATION	75
PHYSICAL PRACTICES	
RESTING AND STOPPING	85
DEEP RELAXATION	91
MINDFUL MOVEMENTS	99
RELATIONSHIP & COMMUNITY PRACTICES	
CREATING AND MAINTAINING A SANGHA	109
BEGINNING ANEW	114
PEACE TREATY	119
SECOND BODY SYSTEM	127
HUGGING MEDITATION	130
DEEP LISTENING AND LOVING SPEECH	134
TAKING CARE OF ANGER AND OTHER STRONG EMOTIONS	138
SHINING LIGHT	149

WRITING A LOVE LETTER	154

EXTENDED PRACTICES

SOLITUDE	159
SILENCE	163
LAZY DAY	166
LISTENING TO A DHARMA TALK	170
DHARMA DISCUSSION	172
TOUCHING THE EARTH	174
TRAVELING AND RETURNING HOME	180
METTA/LOVE MEDITATION	183
UNILATERAL DISARMAMENT	192
TALKING TO YOUR INNER CHILD	196
THE FOURTEEN MINDFULNESS TRAININGS	200

PRACTICING WITH CHILDREN

LISTENING TO YOUR PEOPLE	213
WALKING MEDITATION WITH CHILDREN	217
HELPING CHILDREN WITH ANGER AND OTHER STRONG EMOTIONS	219
FAMILY MEALS	223
INVITING THE BELL	226
PEBBLE MEDITATION	230
THE BREATHING ROOM	235
THE FOUR MANTRAS	239
THE CAKE IN THE REFRIGERATOR	245
ORANGE MEDITATION	248
TREE HUGGING	251
TODAY'S DAY	253
CONCLUSION	255
BACK COVER MATERIAL	261

INTRODUCTION

Mindfulness is the energy of being aware and awake to the present. It is the continuous practice of touching life deeply in every moment. Practicing mindfulness does not require that we go anywhere different. We can practice mindfulness in our room or on our way from one place to another. We can do very much the same things we always do—walking, sitting, working, eating, talking—except we learn to do them with an awareness of what we are doing.

Imagine you're standing with a group of people, contemplating a beautiful sunrise. But while others drink in the view, you struggle. You're preoccupied with your projects and worries. You think about the future and the past. You're not really present to appreciate the experience. So rather than enjoy the sunrise, you let the richness of the moment slip by.

Suppose, instead, you took a different approach. What if, as your mind wanders, you direct your focus to your in-breath and out-breath? As you practice breathing deeply, you bring yourself back to the present. Your body and mind come together as one, allowing you to be fully available to witness, contemplate, and enjoy the scenery. By "going home" to your breath, you regain the wonder of the sunrise.

We often become so busy that we forget what we're doing or who we are. I know many people who say they even forget to breathe. We forget to look at the people we love and to appreciate them until they're gone. Even when we have some leisure time, we don't know how to get in touch with what is going on inside us. So we turn on the television or pick up the telephone as if we might be able to escape from ourselves.

Awareness of the breath is the essence of mindfulness. According to the Buddha, mindfulness is the source of happiness and joy. The seed of mindfulness is in each of us, but we usually forget to water it. If we know how to take refuge in our breath, in our step, then we can touch our seeds of peace and joy and allow them to manifest for our enjoyment. Instead of taking refuge in an abstract notion of God, Buddha, or Allah, we realize that God can be touched in our breath and our step.

This sounds easy, and everyone can do it, but it takes some training. The practice of stopping is crucial. How do we stop? We stop by means of our in-breath, our out-breath, and our step. That is why our basic practice is mindful breathing and mindful walking. If you master these practices, then you can practice mindful eating, mindful drinking, mindful cooking, mindful driving, and so on, and you are always with peace and happiness.

Our practice is the practice of mindfulness—mindfulness of breathing, walking, eating, dishwashing, and cooking—always dwelling in the here and the now and not allowing ourselves to be pulled away by worries, projects for the future, or regrets about the past.

The practice of mindfulness (*smrti* in Sanskrit) leads to concentration (*samadhi*), which in turn leads to insight *(prajña)*. The insight we gain from mindfulness meditation can liberate us from fear, anxiety, and anger, allowing us to be truly happy. We can practice mindfulness using something as simple as a flower. When I hold a flower in my hand, I'm aware of it. My in-breath and out-breath help me maintain my awareness. Rather than becoming overwhelmed by other thoughts, I sustain my enjoyment of the flower's beauty. Concentration itself becomes a source of joy.

If we want to fully enjoy life's gifts, we must practice mindfulness at every turn, whether we're brushing our teeth, cooking our breakfast, or driving to work. Every step and every breath can be an opportunity for joy and happiness. Life is full of suffering. If we don't have enough happiness on reserve, we have no means to take care of our despair. Enjoy your practice with a relaxed and gentle attitude, with an open mind and a receptive heart. Practice for understanding and not for the form or appearance. With mindfulness, we can preserve an inner joy, so that we can better handle the challenges in our lives. We can create a foundation of freedom, peace, and love within ourselves.

DAILY PRACTICES

CONSCIOUS BREATHING

In our daily life, we breathe, but we forget that we're breathing. The foundation of all mindfulness practice is to bring our attention to our in-breath and out-breath. This is called mindfulness of breathing, or conscious breathing. It's very simple, but the effect can be very great. In our daily life, although our body is in one place, our mind is often in another. Paying attention to our in-breath and out-breath brings our mind back to our body. And suddenly we are there, fully present in the here and the now.

Conscious breathing is like drinking a glass of cool water. As we breathe in, we really feel the air filling our lungs. We don't need to control our breath. We feel the breath as it actually is. It may be long or short, deep or shallow. In the light of our awareness it will naturally become slower and deeper. Conscious breathing is the key to uniting body and mind and bringing the energy of mindfulness into each moment of our life.

Regardless of our internal weather—our thoughts, emotions, and perceptions—our breathing is always with us like a faithful friend. Whenever we feel carried away, sunk in a deep emotion, or caught in thoughts about the past or the future, we can return to our breathing to collect and anchor our mind.

Practice

While you breathe in and out, feel the flow of air coming in and going out of your nose. At first your breathing may not be relaxed. But after practicing conscious breathing for awhile, you will feel how light and natural, how calm and peaceful your breathing has become. Any time you're walking, gardening, typing, or doing anything at all, you can return to this peaceful source of life.

You can say to yourself:

Breathing in, I know I'm breathing in.

Breathing out, I know I'm breathing out.

After a few breaths, you may want to shorten this to: "In, Out." If you follow your in-breath and out-breath all the way through, your mind is no longer thinking. Now your mind has a chance to rest. In our daily life we think too much. Giving our mind a chance to stop thinking is wonderful.

Breathing in, I know I'm breathing in isn't a thought. It's a simple awareness that something is happening, that you are breathing in and out. When you breathe in and bring your attention to your in-breath, you bring your mind back to a reunion with your body. Just one in-breath can help the mind come back to the body. When body and mind come together, you can be truly in the present moment.

"Breathing in, I know I'm breathing in" is another way of saying "Breathing in, I feel alive." Life is in you and life is around you—life with all its wonders: the sunshine, the blue sky, the autumn leaves. It's very important to go home to the present moment to get in touch with the healing, refreshing, and nourishing elements of life inside and around you. A light smile can relax all the muscles of your face.

> *Breathing in, I recognize the blue sky.*
> *Breathing out, I smile to the blue sky.*
>
> *Breathing in, I am aware of the beautiful autumn leaves.*
> *Breathing out, I smile to the beautiful autumn leaves.*

You can shorten this to "blue sky" on the in-breath, and "smiling" on the out-breath. Then "autumn leaves" on the in-breath, and "smiling" on the out-breath. When you practice breathing like this, it puts you in touch with all these wonders of life. The beauty of life is nourishing you. You are free from your worries and fears. You get in touch with your breath and with your body. Your body is a wonder. Your eyes are a wonder; you need only to open your eyes to be able to touch the paradise of forms and colors that's available. Your ears are a wonder. Thanks to your ears you can hear all kinds of sounds: music, birdsong, and the wind blowing through the pine trees. When you pay attention to your in-breath and out-breath, you bring yourself home to the present moment, to the here and the now, and you are in touch with life. If you were to continue to be lost in the past or run to the future, you'd miss all of that.

Breathing in, I follow my in-breath all the way through.
Breathing out, I follow my out-breath all the way through.

In the beginning, you may notice that your breathing may feel labored or awkward. Your breath is a result of your body and feelings. If your body has tension or pain, if your feelings are painful, then your breath is affected. Bring your attention to your breath and breathe mindfully.

Breathing in, I know I'm breathing in.
Breathing out, I know I'm breathing out.

> *Breathing in, I smile to my in-breath.*
> *Breathing out, I smile to my out-breath.*

Never force your breath. If your in-breath is short, let it be short. If it's not very peaceful, let it be like that. We don't intervene, force, or "work on" our breath. We just become aware of it, and after some time, the quality of our breathing will improve naturally. Mindfulness of breathing identifies and embraces our in-breath and out-breath, like a mother going home to her child and embracing her child tenderly in her arms. You'll be surprised to see that after one or two minutes, the quality of your breathing will improve. Your in-breath will become deeper; your out-breath will become slower. Your breathing becomes more peaceful and harmonious.

> *Breathing in, I notice that my in-breath has become deeper.*
> *Breathing out, I notice that my out-breath has become slower.*

When you notice that your in-breath and out-breath have become more peaceful, deeper, and slower, you can offer that peace, calm, and harmony to your body. In your daily life, you may neglect and ignore your body. Now is your chance to come home to your body, recognize its existence, get reacquainted, and make friends with it.

Breathing in, I'm aware of my body.
Breathing out, I release all the tension in my body.

These breathing exercises come from the Buddha himself.[1] They're very easy, like child's play. If it's helpful, put your hand on your belly. You'll notice that when you breathe in, your stomach is rising, and when you breathe out, your stomach is falling. Rising, falling. Especially in the lying position, it's easy to feel your abdomen rising and falling. You're aware of your in-breath and out-breath from the beginning to the end. Breathing like this is enjoyable.

---

[1] See Thich Nhat Hanh, Breathe, You Are Alive! (Berkeley, CA: Parallax Press, 2008).

You aren't thinking anymore, of the past, of the future, of your projects, of your suffering. Breathing becomes a pleasure, a reminder of life itself.

> *Breathing in, I enjoy my in-breath.*
> *Breathing out, I enjoy my out-breath.*

Later on, after you've been able to offer that peace and harmony to your body, helping it to release the tension, then you can identify your feelings and emotions.

> *Breathing in, I'm aware of the painful feeling in me.*
> *Breathing out, I smile to the painful feeling in me.*

There's a painful feeling, but there's also mindfulness. Mindfulness is like a mother, embracing the feeling tenderly. Mindfulness is always mindfulness of something. When you breathe mindfully, that is mindfulness of breathing. When you walk mindfully, that is mindfulness of walking. When you drink mindfully, that is mindfulness of drinking. When you're mindful of your feelings, that's mindfulness of feeling. Mindfulness can be brought to intervene in every physical and mental event, bringing recognition and relief.

I'd like to offer you a practice poem you can recite from time to time, while breathing and smiling:

Breathing in, I know I am breathing in.
Breathing out, I know I am breathing out.

As my in-breath grows deep,
My out-breath grows slow.

Breathing in, I calm my body,
Breathing out, I feel at ease.

Breathing in, I smile,
Breathing out, I release.

Dwelling in the present moment,
I know this is a wonderful moment.

You can shorten this to the words below, one word or phrase per breath:
In, Out.
Deep, Slow.
Calm, Ease.
Smile, Release.

Present Moment, Wonderful Moment.

The present moment is the only moment that is real. Your most important task is to be here and now and enjoy the present moment.

SITTING MEDITATION

Sitting meditation is a way for us to return home and give full attention and care to ourselves. Every time we sit down, whether it is in our living room, at the foot of a tree, or on a cushion, we can radiate tranquility like the Buddha sitting on an altar. We bring our full attention to what is within and around us. We let our mind become spacious and our heart soft and kind. With just a few minutes of sitting in this way, we can restore ourselves fully. When we sit down peacefully, breathing and smiling with awareness, we have sovereignty over ourselves.

Sitting meditation is very healing. We can just be with whatever is within us, whether it is pain, anger, irritation, joy, love, or peace. We are with whatever is there without being carried away. We let it come, let it stay, then let it go. We have no need to push, to oppress, or to pretend our thoughts are not there. Instead, we can observe the thoughts and images in our mind with an accepting and loving eye. Despite the storms that arise in us, we're still and calm.

Sitting and breathing, we produce our true presence in the here and the now and offer it to our community and to the world. This is the purpose of sitting: being here, fully alive and fully present.

Practice

Sitting meditation should be a joy. Sit in such a way that you feel happy and relaxed for the entire length of the sitting. Sitting is not hard labor. It's an opportunity to enjoy your own presence, the presence of your family or fellow practitioners, the Earth, the sky, and the cosmos. There's no effort.

If you sit on a cushion, be sure it's the right thickness to support you. You can sit in the full- or half-lotus position, a simple cross-legged position, or however you feel most comfortable. Keep your back straight and your hands folded gently in your lap. If you sit in a chair, be sure your feet are flat on the floor or on a cushion. If your legs or feet fall asleep or begin to hurt during the sitting, just adjust your position mindfully. You can maintain your concentration by following your breathing, and slowly and attentively changing your posture.

Allow all the muscles in your body to relax. Don't fight or struggle. There are people who, after fifteen minutes of sitting meditation, feel pain all over their body because they're making an effort to sit or striving to succeed in their sitting meditation. Just allow yourself to be relaxed, as if you were sitting by the ocean.

While sitting, begin by following your in-breath and out-breath. Whenever a feeling comes up, recognize it. Whenever a thought arises, identify it and recognize it. You can learn a lot from observing what's going on in your body and mind during the sitting meditation. Most of all, sitting is a chance for you to do nothing. You have nothing at all to do; just enjoy sitting and breathing in and out.

Breathing in, I know I'm alive.

Breathing out, I smile to life, in me and around me.

Being alive is a miracle. Just sitting there, enjoying your in-breath and out-breath is already happiness. Since you're breathing in and out, you know that you're alive. That's something worth celebrating. So sitting meditation is a way to celebrate life with your in-breath and your out-breath.

It's important to allow your body to relax completely. Don't try to become a buddha. Just enjoy sitting and accept yourself as you are. Even if there's some tension in your body, some pain in your heart, accept yourself like that. With the energy of mindfulness of breathing, you embrace your body and your mind, you allow yourself to be in a relaxed position and enjoy your breathing.

Breathing in, I have arrived.
Breathing out, I feel at home.

You don't need to run anymore. Your true home is in the here and the now. You are solid and free. You can smile, relaxing all the muscles in your face.

We need some training to be successful in our sitting. We're so used to always doing something—with our mind, with our body—that sitting down and doing nothing can be difficult at first. When Nelson Mandela came to France to visit French president Francois Mitterrand, the press asked Mr. Mandela what he'd like to do the most. He said, "What I want to do the most is to just sit down and do nothing. Since my release from prison, I've been so busy with no time to sit or breathe. So what I want the most is just to sit down and not do anything."

If we gave Nelson Mandela a few days to sit and do nothing, would he know how to do it? Because sitting and doing nothing doesn't seem to be very easy for most of us. We're used to always doing something. We need some training to be able to sit and enjoy the sitting, to do nothing and enjoy doing nothing. Each of us has the habit energy of always having to be doing something. If we're not doing something, we can't stand it. So just sitting down and doing nothing is an art, the art of sitting meditation.

If you're having trouble concentrating, counting is an excellent technique. Breathing in, count "one." Breathing out, count "one." Breathing in, count "two." Breathing out, count "two." Continue up to ten and then start counting over again. If at any time you forget where you are, begin again with "one." The method of counting helps us refrain from dwelling on troublesome thoughts; instead we concentrate on our breathing and the number. When we have developed some control over our thinking, counting may become tedious and we can abandon it and just follow the breath.

If you approach meditation as a fight to arrive somewhere and you try hard to achieve success, you won't be able to relax. Look out the window. Perhaps there is a linden tree or an oak tree out there. The tree is beautiful and healthy, being entirely itself. It doesn't seem that the tree is making any effort at all. It allows itself to be—fresh, green, stable. Perhaps the tree is on a mountain. The mountain is strong and solid, supporting all kinds of life without strain or effort. When you practice sitting meditation, you are stable and solid like a mountain. You can practice like this:

Breathing in, I see myself as a mountain.
Breathing out, I enjoy my solidity.

To succeed in your sitting, release the tension in your body and in your feelings. Get comfortable in your seated body. When you begin to breathe in and out, enjoy the breathing in, the breathing out. Give up any struggle and enjoy sitting and smiling. This is a privileged moment, having the opportunity to sit quietly like this. You are your own island. Nobody at this moment can ask you to do anything. Nobody will disturb you, no one has the right to ask you a question, or to ask you to go and wash the pots or clean the bathroom. This is your precious opportunity to relax and be yourself.

WALKING MEDITATION

The mind can go in a thousand directions.
But on this beautiful path, I walk in peace.
With each step, a gentle wind blows.
With each step, a flower blooms.

We walk all the time, but usually it's more like running. Our hurried steps print anxiety and sorrow on the earth. If we can take one step in peace, we can take two, three, four, and then five steps for the peace and happiness of humankind and the Earth.

Walking meditation is walking just to enjoy walking. Walking without arriving, that is the technique. There is a Sanskrit word, *apranihita*. It means wishlessness or aimlessness. The idea is that we do not put anything ahead of ourselves and run after it. When we practice walking meditation, we walk in this spirit. We just enjoy the walking, with no particular aim or destination.

Our walking is not a means to an end. We walk for the sake of walking.

Our mind tends to dart from one thing to another, like a monkey swinging from branch to branch without stopping to rest. Thoughts have millions of pathways, and they forever pull us along into the world of forgetfulness. If we can transform our walking path into a field for meditation, our feet will take every step in full awareness. Our breathing will be in harmony with our steps, and our mind will naturally be at ease. Every step we take will reinforce our peace and joy and cause a stream of calm energy to flow through us. Then we can say, "With each step, a gentle wind blows."

You can practice walking meditation anytime you walk, even if it's only from the car to the office or from the kitchen to the living room. When you walk anywhere, allow enough time to practice; instead of three minutes, give yourself eight or ten. I always leave for the airport an extra hour early so I can practice walking meditation there. Friends want to keep me until the last minute, but I resist. I tell them that I need the time. Walking meditation is like eating. With each step, we nourish our body and our spirit. When we walk with anxiety and sorrow, it's a kind of junk food. The food of walking meditation should be of a higher quality. Just walk slowly and enjoy a banquet of peace.

A.J. Muste said, "There is no way to peace; peace is the way." Walking in mindfulness brings us peace and joy, and makes our life real. Why rush? Our final destination will only be the cemetery. Why not walk in the direction of life, enjoying peace in each moment with every step? There is no need to struggle. Enjoy every step you make. Every step brings you home to the here and the now. This is your true home—because only in this moment, in this place, can life be possible. We have already arrived.

The Earth is our mother. When we are away from mother nature for too long, we get sick. Each step we take in walking meditation allows us to touch our mother, so that we can be well again. A lot of harm has been done to mother earth, so now it is time to kiss the earth with our feet and heal our mother.

Some of us may not be able to walk. When we practice walking meditation at our retreats, each person who can't walk chooses someone who is practicing walking meditation to watch and become one with, following her steps in mindfulness. In this way, he makes peaceful and serene steps together with his partner, even though he himself cannot walk.

We who have two legs must not forget to be grateful. We walk for ourselves, and we walk for those who cannot walk. We walk for all living beings—past, present, and future.

Practice

When you begin to practice walking meditation, you might feel unbalanced, like a baby taking her first steps. Follow your breathing, dwell mindfully on your steps, and soon you will find your balance. Visualize a tiger walking slowly, and you will find that your steps become as majestic as hers.

You may like to start by practicing walking meditation in the morning, allowing the energy of the pure morning air to enter you. Your movements will become smooth and your mind will become alert. Throughout the day, you will find you have a heightened awareness of your actions. When you make decisions after walking meditation, you will find that you are more calm and clear, and have more insight and compassion. With each peaceful step you take, all beings, near and far, will benefit.

As you walk, pay attention to each step you make. Walk slowly. Don't rush. Each step brings you into the best moment of your life. In walking meditation, you practice being aware of the number of steps you make with each breath. Notice each breath and how many steps you take as you breathe in and breathe out. In walking meditation we match our steps to our breath, and not the other way around. When you breathe in, take two or three steps, depending on the capacity of your lungs. If your lungs want two steps while breathing in, then give exactly two steps. If you feel better with three steps, then give yourself three steps. When you breathe out, also listen to your lungs. Know how many steps your lungs want you to make while breathing out.

When you first start practicing, your in-breath is usually shorter than your out-breath. So, you might start your practice with two steps for the in-breath and three for the out-breath: 2-3; 2-3; 2-3. Or, 3-4; 3-4; 3-4. But later on it may become more even: 2-2 or 3-3. As we continue, our breathing naturally becomes slower and more relaxed. If you feel you need to make one more step while breathing in, then allow yourself to enjoy that. Whenever you feel that you want to make one more step while breathing out, then allow your-self to have one more step breathing out. Every step should be enjoyable.

Don't try to control your breathing. Allow your lungs as much time and air as they need, and simply notice how many steps you take as your lungs fill up and how many you take as they empty, being mindful of both your breath and your steps. The link is the counting.

When you walk uphill or downhill, the number of steps per breath will change. Always follow the needs of your lungs. Observe them deeply. Don't forget to practice smiling. Your half-smile will bring calm and delight to your steps and your breath, and help sustain your attention. After practicing for half an hour or an hour, you will find that your breath, your steps, your counting, and your half-smile come together easily.

After some time of practice, you will find that the in-breath and the out-breath will become closer in length. Your lungs will be healthier, and your blood will circulate better. Your way of breathing will have been transformed.

We can practice walking meditation by counting steps or by using words. If the rhythm of our breathing is 3-3, for example, we can say, silently, "Lotus flower blooms. Lotus flower blooms," or "The green planet. The green planet," as we walk. If our breathing rhythm is 2-3, we might say, "Lotus flower. Lotus flower blooms." If we are taking five in-breaths and five out-breaths, we may say: "Walking on the green planet. Walking on the green planet." Or "Walking on the green planet, I'm walking on the green planet," for 5-6.

We don't just say the words. We really see flowers blooming under our feet. We really become one with our green planet. Feel free to use your own creativity and wisdom to create your own words. Here are some that I wrote:

> *Peace is every step.*
> *The shining red sun is my heart.*
> *Each flower smiles with me.*
> *How green, how fresh all that grows.*
> *How cool the wind blows.*
> *Peace is every step.*
> *It turns the endless path to joy.*

Every day, you walk somewhere, so adding walking meditation to your life doesn't take a lot of additional time or require you to go anywhere different. Choose a place—a staircase, your driveway, or the distance from one tree to another—to do walking meditation every day. Every path can be a walking meditation path.

WAKING UP

We can start our day with the happiness of a smile and the aspiration to dedicate ourselves to the path of love and understanding. We are aware that today is a fresh, new day, and we have twenty-four precious hours to live.

Practice

As you wake up in the morning and open your eyes, you may like to recite this *gatha:*

*Waking up this morning, I smile.
Twenty-four brand-new hours are before me.
I vow to live fully in each moment and to look at all beings with eyes of compassion.*

The last line of this gatha comes from the Lotus Sutra.[2] The one who looks at all beings with eyes of

---

[2] See Thich Nhat Hanh, Peaceful Action, Open Heart: Insights on the Lotus Sutra (Berkeley, CA: Parallax Press, 2008).

compassion is Avalokiteshvara, the bodhisattva who listens deeply to the cries of the world. In the sutra, this line reads: "Eyes of loving kindness look on all living beings." Love is impossible without understanding. In order to understand others, we must know them and be inside their skin. Then we can treat them with loving kindness. The source of love is our fully awakened mind.

After you wake up, you probably open the curtains and look outside. You may even like to open the window and feel the cool morning air with the dew still on the grass. When you open the window and look out, see that life is infinitely marvelous. At that very moment, you can vow to be awake all day long, realizing joy, peace, freedom, and harmony. When you do this, your mind becomes clear like a calm river.

Try to get up from bed right away after enjoying three deep breaths to bring yourself into mindfulness. Don't delay waking. You may like to sit up and gently massage your head, neck, shoulders, and arms to get your blood circulating. You might like to do a few stretches to loosen your joints and wake up your body. Drinking a cup of warm water is also good for our system first thing in the morning.

Wash yourself or do what you need to before heading to work or school or to the meditation hall. Allow enough time so you don't have to rush. If it's still early, enjoy the dark morning sky. Many stars are twinkling and greeting us. Take deep breaths and enjoy the cool, fresh air. As you walk slowly to the car, to school, to work, or to the meditation hall, let the morning fill your being, awakening your body and mind to the joy of a new day.

What better way to start the day than with a smile? Your smile affirms your awareness and determination to live in peace and joy. How many days slip by in forgetfulness? What are you doing with your life? Look deeply, and smile. The source of a true smile is an awakened mind.

How can you remember to smile when you wake up? You might hang a reminder—such as a branch, a leaf, a painting, or some inspiring words—in your window or from the ceiling above your bed. Once you develop the practice of smiling, you may not need a sign. You will smile as soon as you hear a bird sing or see the sunlight stream through the window, and this will help you approach the day with more gentleness and understanding.

THE BELL

Sometimes we need a sound to remind us to return to our conscious breathing, we call these sounds "bells of mindfulness." In Plum Village and the other practice centers in my tradition, we stop whenever we hear the telephone ringing, the clock chiming, or the monastery bell sounding. These are our bells of mindfulness. When we hear the sound of the bell, we stop talking and stop moving. We relax our body and become aware of our breathing. We do it naturally, with enjoyment, and without solemnity or stiffness. When we stop to breathe and restore our calm and our peace, we become free, our work becomes more enjoyable, and the friend in front of us becomes more real.

Sometimes our bodies may be home, but we're not truly home. Our mind is elsewhere. The bell can help bring the mind back to the body. That's how we practice in a temple. Because the bell can help us to go back to ourselves, back to the present moment, we consider the bell to be a friend, a bodhisattva that helps us to wake up to ourselves again.

At home, we can use the ringing of the telephone, the local church bells, the cry of a baby, or even the sound of a siren or a car alarm as our bells of mindfulness. With just three conscious breaths we can release the tension in our body and mind and return to a cool, clear state of being.

In Vietnam, I was used to hearing the sound of the Buddhist temple bell. When I came to the West there was no Buddhist bell; I only heard the church bell. One day when I'd been in Europe for several years, I was doing walking meditation in Prague. Suddenly I heard the sound of the church bell, and for the first time I was able to touch deeply the soul of ancient Europe. Since then, every time I hear the church bell, whether it's in Switzerland or France or Russia, I deeply touch the soul of Europe. For those of us who don't train ourselves, the sound of the bell doesn't mean much. But if we train ourselves, the sound will have a very spiritual meaning for us, and will wake up the most wonderful things inside us.

In our tradition, we don't say "striking" the bell; we say "inviting the bell to sound." And the person who invites the bell is the bell master. We call the wooden stick that invites the bell, "the inviter." There are many kinds of bells: big bells that can be heard by the whole village or neighborhood; smaller bells that announce activities and can be heard all over the practice center; the bowl bell in the meditation hall that helps us with the practice of breathing and sitting; and then there is the minibell, one of the smallest bells: it fits in a pocket and we can bring it along with us wherever we go.

It's very important to train ourselves to be able to invite the bell. If we're solid, awake, free, very mindful, then the sound of the bell that we offer can help people touch what is deepest within them.

Practice

When you're a bell master and you want to invite the bell to sound, the first thing you do is bow to the bell. The bell is like a friend who helps you bring your mind back to your body. When mind and body are together, suddenly we're in the here and now, and we can live our life deeply.

If you have a small bell that fits in your hand, after you bow to the bell, take the small bell and hold it in your open palm. Imagine that your hand is a lotus flower with five petals, and the small bell is like a jewel in the lotus flower. While you hold the bell like this, you practice mindful breathing in and out. There's a poem that helps you to bring your mind back to your body so that you can be truly present. If you are not truly present in the here and the now, you can't be a good bell master. So after having breathed in and out two times with this poem, you're qualified to be a bell master.

> *Body, speech, and mind in perfect oneness,*
> *I send my heart along with the sound of this bell.*
> *May the hearers awaken from forgetfulness*
> *and transcend the path of anxiety and sorrow.*

Four lines: one line for breathing in, one line for breathing out, one line for breathing in, one line for breathing out. If you don't remember the gatha, it's okay. You can just breathe in and enjoy your in-breath, and breathe out and enjoy your out-breath. That will make you into a bell master also. But the gatha is very beautiful. You are now ready to invite the bell to sound.

Make a half-sound in order to wake the bell up, gently. It's a very important warning to the bell and the people. You're being gentle to the bell so that it doesn't have a surprise. And you want to warn people that a full sound of the bell is coming, so they can prepare themselves to receive it with their true presence. In a practice center, the sound of the bell is like the voice of the Buddha from within us, calling us home. When you wake up the bell, people will stop their thinking and their talking, and will go back to their breathing while they wait for the sound of the bell. You have to allow them enough time to prepare themselves for the full sound of the bell, so you give them the time of one in-breath and one out-breath to be ready. They may be excited, saying something, or thinking about something. But when they hear the half sound, they know they should stop—stop thinking, stop talking, stop doing things—and prepare themselves to be ready to hear the bell.

Then you invite the bell to sound a full sound. Breathe in and out deeply three times. If you enjoy breathing in and enjoy breathing out, then after three in-breaths and three out-breaths you become relaxed, calm, serene, mindful. You can recite this poem to yourself as you breathe in and out:

Listen, listen.
This wonderful sound
brings me back
to my true home.

"Listen, listen" means listen with all your heart when you breathe in. "My true home" is life, with all its wonders that are available in the here and the now. If you practice well, the Kingdom of God and the Pure Land of the Buddha will be available whenever you go home to yourself with the sound of the bell.

TELEPHONE MEDITATION

Don't underestimate the effect your words have when you use right speech. The words we speak can build up understanding and love. They can be as beautiful as gems, as lovely as flowers, and they can make many people happy. But often, when we speak on the phone, we are too busy doing too many things at once to focus on our speech.

The telephone is a very convenient means of communication, and the cell phone even more so. It can save us travel time and expense. But the telephone can also tyrannize us. If it is always ringing, we are disturbed and cannot accomplish much. If we talk on the phone without awareness, we waste precious time and money. Often we say things that are not important, while around us are all the joys of the present moment: a child wanting to hold our hand, a bird singing, the sun shining.

When the telephone rings, the bell creates in us a kind of vibration, maybe some anxiety: "Who is calling? Is it good news or bad news?" There is a force that pulls us to the phone. We cannot resist. We can become the victim of our own telephone.

Practice

The next time your phone rings, stay exactly where you are, and become aware of your breathing: "Breathing in, I calm my body. Breathing out, I smile." When the phone rings the second time, breathe again. When it rings the third time, continue practicing breathing, and then pick up the phone. Remember, you can be your own master, moving like a buddha, dwelling in mindfulness. When you pick up the phone, you are smiling, not only for your own sake, but also for the sake of the other person. If you are irritated or angry, the other person will receive your negativity. But since you are smiling, how fortunate for her!

Before you make a phone call, breathe in and out twice, and recite this verse:

Words can travel thousands of miles.
May my words create mutual understanding and love.
May they be as beautiful as gems, as lovely as flowers.

Then pick up the phone and dial. When the bell rings, perhaps your friend is breathing and smiling and won't pick up the phone until the third ring. Continue to practice: "Breathing in, I calm my body. Breathing out, I smile." Both of you are on your phones, breathing and smiling. This is very beautiful! You don't have to go into a meditation hall to do this wonderful practice. It is available in your house or office. Practicing telephone meditation can counteract stress and depression and bring the Buddha into your daily life.

BOWING

When we greet someone with a bow, we have the chance to be present with that person and acknowledge the capacity for full awareness within us and within the other person. We don't bow just to be polite or diplomatic, but to recognize the miracle of being alive and the potential each person has to be awake. To bow or not to bow is not the question. The important thing is to be mindful.

Practice

When we see someone join his or her palms to bow to us, we can do the same. Joining our palms and breathing in, we silently say, "A lotus for you." Bowing our head and breathing out, we say, "A buddha to be." We do this in mindfulness, truly aware that the person is there in front of us. We bow with all our sincerity of our heart. Sometimes, when we feel a deep connection to what is there in front of us, a sense of awe at the wonders of life—whether that be a flower, a sunset, a tree, or the cool drops of rain—we might like to bow in this way as well, to offer our presence and gratitude.

When we bow to the Buddha we are really acknowledging the capacity to be awake inherent within ourselves. Paying respect to the Buddha, when understood and practiced in this way, is not merely devotional but also a wisdom practice. When we bow to the great bodhisattvas, we touch deeply the qualities they represent and feel deep gratitude for those who follow their example. In showing respect for the great bodhisattvas, we're also demonstrating our commitment to practice the bodhisattva path and cultivate the energy of understanding, love, and compassion in ourselves. Bowing in this spirit is a practice of meditation.

GATHAS

Breathing, sitting, and walking meditation are wonderful, but in our daily life we can be so busy that we forget our intention to breathe or walk mindfully. One way to help us dwell in the present moment is to practice with gathas or mindfulness verses. Gathas are short verses that help us practice mindfulness in our daily activities. A gatha can open and deepen our experience of simple acts that we often take for granted. Focusing our mind on a gatha, we return to ourselves and become more aware of each action. When the gatha ends, we continue our activity with heightened awareness. At Plum Village, where I live in France, we practice gathas when we wake up, when we enter the meditation hall, during meals, and when we wash the dishes. In fact, we recite gathas silently throughout the entire day to help us attend to the present moment.

When we drive a car, signs can help us find our way. When we see a sign, it can guide us along the way until the next sign. When we practice with gathas, the gathas can guide our daily activities, and we can live our entire day in awareness.

Practice

When you turn on the water faucet, look deeply and see how precious the water is. Remember not to waste a single drop because there are so many people in the world who don't have enough to drink.

Water flows from high mountains.
Water runs deep in the Earth.
Miraculously water comes to us
and sustains all life.

While brushing your teeth, you can make a vow to use loving speech with this gatha:

Brushing my teeth and rinsing my mouth,
I vow to speak purely and lovingly.
When my mouth is fragrant with right speech,
a flower blooms in the garden of my heart.

Before turning on the engine of your car, you can prepare for a safe journey by reciting the gatha for starting the car:

Before starting the car
I know where I am going.
The car and I are one.
If the car goes fast, I go fast.

The gatha brings your mind and body together. With a calm and clear mind, fully aware of the activities of your body, you are less likely to get into a car accident.

Gathas are nourishment for your mind and body, giving you peace, calm, and joy, which you can share with others. They help you to bring the uninterrupted practice of meditation into every part of your day. You can start with the gathas here, find more in the book *Present Moment Wonderful Moment,* or you can write your own.[3]

---

[3] See Thich Nhat Hanh, Present Moment Wonderful Moment: Mindfulness Verses for Daily Living and Present Moment Wonderful Moment: 52 Inspirational Cards and a Companion Book (Berkeley, CA: Parallax Press, 2006).

Writing your own gathas is a longstanding Zen tradition, one that I inherited from my teacher and pass on to my students.

I HAVE ARRIVED, I AM HOME

Imagine you are on a plane flying to New York. Once you sit down on the plane, you think, "I have to sit here for six hours before I arrive." Sitting in the plane you think only of New York, and you are not able to live the moments that are offered to you now. But it is possible for you to walk on to the plane in such a way that you enjoy every step. You don't need to arrive in New York in order to be peaceful and happy. As you walk on to the plane, every step brings you happiness, and you arrive in every moment. To arrive means to arrive somewhere. When we practice walking meditation, we arrive in every moment—we arrive at the destination of life. The present moment is a destination. Breathing in, I make a step and another step, and I tell myself, "I have arrived, I have arrived."

"I have arrived" is our practice. When we breathe in, we take refuge in our in-breath, and we say, "I have arrived." When we make a step, we take refuge in our step, and we say, "I have arrived." This is not a statement to yourself or another person. "I have arrived" means I have stopped running, I have arrived in the present moment, because only the present moment contains life. When I breathe in and take refuge in my in-breath, I touch life deeply. When I take a step and I take refuge entirely in my step, I also touch life deeply, and by doing so I stop running.

Stopping running is a very important practice. We have been running all our life. We believe that peace, happiness, and success are present in some other place and time. We don't know that everything—peace, happiness, and stability—should be looked for in the here and the now. This is the address of life—the intersection of here and now.

When we practice this meditation, we arrive in each moment. Our true home is in the present moment. When we enter the present moment deeply, our regrets and sorrows disappear, and we discover life with all its wonders.

Practice

I have arrived. I am home.
In the here, in the now.
I am solid. I am free.
In the ultimate, I dwell.

This verse is wonderful to practice during walking meditation. As you breathe in, you say, "Arrived" with each step, and as you breathe out, you say "Home" with each step. If your rhythm is 2-3, you will say, "Arrived, arrived. Home, home, home," coordinating the words and your steps according to the rhythm of your breathing.

After practicing "Arrived/Home" for a while, if you feel relaxed and fully present with each step and each breath, you can switch to "Here/Now." The words are different, but the practice is the same.

This verse also works well in sitting meditation. Breathing in, we say to ourselves, "I have arrived." Breathing out, we say, "I am home." When we do this, we overcome dispersion and dwell peacefully in the present moment, which is the only moment for us to be alive.

"I have arrived" is a practice, not a statement or declaration. I have arrived in the here and the now, and I can touch life deeply with all of its wonders. The rain is a wonder; the sunshine is a wonder; the trees are a wonder; the faces of children are a wonder. There are so many wonders of life around you and inside you. Your eyes are a wonder; you need only to open them to see all kinds of colors and forms. Your heart is a wonder; if your heart stops beating, then nothing can continue.

When you go home to the present moment, you touch the wonders of life that are inside you and around you. Just enjoy this moment; you don't have to wait for tomorrow to have peace and joy. When you breathe in you say, "I have arrived," and you will know whether you have arrived or not, you will know whether you are still running or not. Even sitting quietly, you may still be running in your mind. When you feel you have arrived, you will be very happy. You must tell your friend, "Dear friend, I have really arrived." This is good news.

TAKING REFUGE

When we find ourselves in dangerous or difficult situations, or when we feel like we are losing ourselves, we can practice taking refuge. Instead of panicking or giving ourselves up to despair, we can put our trust in the power of self-healing, self-understanding, and loving within us. We call this the island within ourselves in which we can take refuge. It is an island of peace, confidence, solidity, love, and freedom. Be an island within yourself. You don't have to look for it elsewhere.

We want to feel safe and protected. We want to feel calm. So when a situation seems to be turbulent, overwhelming, full of suffering, we have to practice taking refuge in the Buddha, the Buddha in ourselves. Each of us has the seed of buddhahood, the capacity for being calm, understanding, compassionate, and for taking refuge in the island of safety within us so we can maintain our humanness, our peace, our hope. Practicing like this, we become an island of peace and compassion, and we may inspire others to do the same.

Practice

Use this gatha to return to yourself, wherever you are:

Breathing in, I go back to the island within myself.
There are beautiful trees within the island.
There are cool streams of water, there are birds, sunshine, and fresh air.
Breathing out, I feel safe.

We are like a boat crossing the ocean. If the boat encounters a storm and everyone panics, the boat will turn over. If there is one person in the boat who can remain calm, that person can inspire other people to be calm. Then there will be hope for the whole boatload. Who is that person who can stay calm in the situation of distress? Each of us is that person. We count on each other.

THE FIVE MINDFULNESS TRAINING

The Five Mindfulness Trainings are one of the most concrete ways to practice mindfulness. They are nonsectarian and their nature is universal. They are really the practices of compassion and understanding. All spiritual traditions have their equivalent to the five mindfulness trainings as guidelines, signposts for how to respond to all of the varied and sometimes unhealthy choices that are available in our society.

The first training is to protect life, to decrease violence in one-self, in the family, and in society. The second training is to practice social justice, generosity, not stealing, and not exploiting other living beings. The third is the practice of responsible sexual behavior in order to protect individuals, couples, families, and children. The fourth is the practice of deep listening and loving speech to restore communication and for reconciliation to take place. The fifth is about mindful consumption, to help us not bring toxins and poisons into our body, our mind; not to consume television, magazines, films, and so on that contain a lot of poisons like violence, craving, and hatred.

The Five Mindfulness Trainings are based on the precepts developed during the time of the Buddha to be the foundation of practice for the entire lay practice community.

I have translated these precepts for modern times as The Five Mindfulness Trainings because mindfulness is at the foundation of each one of them. With mindfulness, we are aware of what is going on in our bodies, our feelings, our minds, and the world, and we avoid doing harm to ourselves and others. Mindfulness protects us, our families, and our society, and ensures a safe and happy present and a safe and happy future. When we are mindful, we can see that by refraining from doing this, we prevent that from happening. We arrive at our own unique insight, not something imposed on us by an outside authority. It is the fruit of our own observation. Practicing the mindfulness trainings, therefore, helps us be more calm and concentrated and brings more insight and enlightenment, which makes our practice of the mindfulness trainings more solid.

In the practice centers in my tradition, both monastic and lay-people agree to observe these trainings to support our practice of mindfulness and living harmoniously together. No smoking, no drinking alcohol, and no sexual misconduct constitute part of The Five Mindfulness Trainings to be observed at our practice centers.

Anyone at any time can decide to live by The Five Mindfulness Trainings. When we practice The Five Mindfulness Trainings, we become bodhisattvas helping to create harmony, protect the environment, safeguard peace, and cultivate brotherhood and sister-hood. Not only do we safeguard the beauties of our own culture but those of other cultures as well, and all the beauties of the Earth. With The Five Mindfulness Trainings in our hearts, we are already on the path of transformation and healing.

Practice

THE FIRST TRAINING Aware of the suffering caused by the destruction of life, I vow to cultivate compassion and learn ways to protect the lives of people, animals, plants, and minerals. I am determined not to kill, not to let others kill, and not to condone any act of killing in the world, in my thinking, and in my way of life.

THE SECOND TRAINING Aware of the suffering caused by exploitation, social injustice, stealing, and oppression, I vow to cultivate loving kindness and learn ways to work for the well-being of people, animals, plants, and minerals. I vow to practice generosity by sharing my time, energy, and material resources with those in real need. I am determined not to steal and not to possess anything that should belong to others. I will respect the property of others, but I will prevent others from profiting from human suffering or the suffering of other species on Earth.

THE THIRD TRAINING Aware of the suffering caused by sexual misconduct, I vow to cultivate responsibility and learn ways to protect the safety and integrity of individuals, couples, families, and society. I am determined not to engage in sexual relations without love and a long-term commitment. To preserve the happiness of myself and others, I am determined to respect my commitments and the commitments of others. I will do everything in my power to protect children from sexual abuse and to prevent couples and families from being broken by sexual misconduct.

THE FOURTH TRAINING Aware of the suffering caused by unmindful speech and the inability to listen to others, I vow to cultivate loving speech and deep listening in order to bring joy and happiness to others and relieve others of suffering. Knowing that words can create happiness or suffering, I vow to learn to speak truthfully, with words that inspire self-confidence, joy, and hope. I am determined not to spread news that I do not know to be certain and not to criticize or condemn things of which I am not sure. I will refrain from uttering words that can cause division or discord, or words that can cause the family or the community to break. I will make all efforts to reconcile and resolve all conflicts, however small.

THE FIFTH TRAINING Aware of the suffering caused by unmindful consumption, I vow to cultivate good health, both physical and mental, for myself, my family, and my society by practicing mindful eating, drinking, and consuming. I vow to ingest only items that preserve peace, well-being, and joy in my body, in my consciousness, and in the collective body and consciousness of my family and society. I am determined not to use alcohol or any other intoxicant or to ingest foods or other items that contain toxins, such as certain TV programs, magazines, books, films, and conversations. I am aware that to damage my body and my consciousness with these poisons is to betray my ancestors, my parents, my society, and future generations. I will work to transform violence, fear, anger, and confusion in myself and in society by practicing a diet for myself and for society. I understand that a proper diet is crucial for self-transformation and the transformation of society.

EATING PRACTICES

MINDFUL EATING

The bread in my hand is the body of the cosmos.

Eating is a meditative practice. We should try to offer our full presence for every meal. As we serve our food, we can already begin practicing. Serving ourselves, we realize that many elements, such as the rain, sunshine, earth, and the care taken by the farmers and the cooks, have all come together to form this wonderful meal. In fact, through this food we see that the entire universe is supporting our existence.

Having the opportunity to sit and enjoy wonderful food is something precious, something not everyone has. Many people in the world are hungry. When I hold a bowl of rice or a piece of bread, I know that I am fortunate, and I feel compassion for all those who have no food to eat and are without friends or family. This is a very deep practice. We do not need to go to a temple or a church in order to practice this. We can practice it right at our dinner table. Mindful eating can cultivate seeds of compassion and understanding that will strengthen us to do something to help hungry and lonely people be nourished.

Practice

Eating a meal in mindfulness is an important practice. Turn off the TV, put down the newspaper, and work together for five or ten minutes, setting the table and finishing whatever needs to be done. During these few minutes, you can be very happy. When the food is on the table and everyone is seated, practice breathing: "Breathing in, I calm my body. Breathing out, I smile," three times.

Then, look at each person as you breathe in and out in order to be in touch with yourself and everyone at the table. You don't need two hours in order to see another person. If you are really settled within yourself, you only need to look for one or two seconds, and that is enough to see your friend or family member. I think that if a family has five members, only about five or ten seconds is needed to practice this "looking and seeing."

After breathing, smile. Sitting at the table with other people is a chance to offer an authentic smile of friendship and understanding. It is very easy, but not many people do it. To me, the most important part of the practice is to look at each person and smile. If the people eating together cannot smile at each other, the situation is a very dangerous one.

After breathing and smiling, look down at the food in a way that allows the food to become real. This food reveals your connection with the Earth. Each bite contains the life of the sun and the Earth. The extent to which our food reveals itself depends on us. You can see and taste the whole universe in a piece of bread! Contemplating your food for a few seconds before eating, and eating in mindfulness, can bring you much happiness.

Upon finishing your meal, take a few moments to notice that you have finished, your bowl is now empty and your hunger is satisfied. You can take a moment to be grateful that you have had this nourishing food to eat, supporting you on the path of love and understanding.

The meal is finished, my hunger satisfied,
I vow to live for the benefit of all beings.

From time to time, you might want to try the practice of eating in silence with your family or friends. Eating in silence allows us to see the preciousness of the food and our friends, and also our close relationship with the Earth and all species. Every vegetable, every drop of water, every piece of bread contains in it the life of our whole planet and the sun. With each bite of food, we can taste the meaning and value of our life. We can meditate on the plants and animals, on the work of the farmer, and on the many thousands of children who die each day for lack of food. Sitting silently at the table with others, we also have the opportunity to see them clearly and deeply, and to smile to communicate real love and friendship. The first time you eat in silence, it may seem awkward, but after you get used to it, silent meals can bring a lot of peace, joy, and insight. It's like turning off the TV before eating. We "turn off" the talking sometimes in order to enjoy the food and the presence of one another.

I do not recommend silent meals every day. I think talking to each other is a wonderful way to be in touch. But we have to distinguish among different kinds of talk. Some subjects can separate us, for instance if we talk about other people's shortcomings. The food that has been prepared carefully will have no value if we let this kind of talk dominate our meal. When instead we speak about things that nourish our awareness of the food and our being together, we cultivate the kind of happiness that is necessary for us to grow. If we compare this experience with the experience of talking about other people's shortcomings, I think awareness of a piece of bread in your mouth is a much more nourishing experience. It brings life in and makes life real.

I propose that during eating, you refrain from discussing subjects that can destroy your awareness of the family and the food. But you should feel free to say things that can nourish awareness and happiness. For instance, if there's a dish that you like very much, you can see if other people are also enjoying it, and if one of them is not, you can help her appreciate the wonderful dish prepared with loving care. If someone is thinking about something other than the good food on the table, such as his difficulties in the office or with friends, it means he is losing the present moment, and the food. You can say, "This dish is wonderful, don't you agree?" When you say something like this, you will draw him out of his thinking and worries, and bring him back to the here and now, enjoying you, enjoying the wonderful dish. You become a bodhisattva, helping a living being become enlightened.

In our practice centers, we invite the bell three times before eating, and then we eat in silence for about twenty minutes. Eating in silence, we are fully aware of our food's nourishment. In order to deepen our practice of mindful eating and support the peaceful atmosphere, we remain seated during this silent period. At the end of this time, two sounds of the bell will be invited. We may then start a mindful conversation with our friend or begin to get up from the table.

THE FIVE CONTEMPLATIONS

Contemplating our food for a few seconds before eating and eating in mindfulness can bring us much happiness. In our practice centers, we use the Five Contemplations as a way of reminding us where our food comes from and its purpose.

The first contemplation is being aware that our food comes directly from the earth and sky. It is a gift of the earth and sky, and also of the people who prepared it. The second contemplation is about being worthy of the food we eat. The way to be worthy of our food is to eat mindfully—to be aware of its presence and thankful for having it. We cannot allow ourselves to get lost in our worries, fears, or anger over the past or the future. We are there for the food because the food is there for us; it is only fair. Eat in mindfulness, and you will be worthy of the earth and the sky.

The third contemplation is about becoming aware of our negative tendencies and not allowing them to carry us away. We need to learn how to eat in moderation, to eat the right amount of food. The bowl that is used by a monk or a nun is referred to as the "instrument of appropriate measure." It is very important not to overeat. If you eat slowly and chew very carefully, you will get plenty of nutrition. The right amount of food is the amount that helps us stay healthy.

The fourth contemplation is about the quality of our food. We are determined to ingest only food that has no toxins for our body and our consciousness, food that keeps us healthy and nourishes our compassion. This is mindful eating. The Buddha said that if you eat in such a way that compassion is destroyed in you, it is like eating the flesh of your own children. So practice eating in such a way that you can keep compassion alive in you.

The fifth contemplation is being aware that we receive food in order to realize something. Our lives should have meaning and that meaning is to help people suffer less, and help them to touch the joys of life. When we have compassion in our hearts and know that we are able to help a person suffer less, life begins to have more meaning. This is very important food for us and can bring us a lot of joy. A single person is capable of helping many living beings. And it is something we can do anywhere.

Practice

THE FIRST CONTEMPLATION This food is a gift of the whole universe, the earth, the sky, and much mindful work.

THE SECOND CONTEMPLATION May we eat in mindfulness so as to be worthy of it.

THE THIRD CONTEMPLATION May we transform our unskillful states of mind and learn to eat in moderation.

THE FOURTH CONTEMPLATION May we take only foods that nourish us and prevent illness.

THE FIFTH CONTEMPLATION May we accept this food to realize the path of understanding and love.

THE KITCHEN

In these fresh vegetables
I see a green sun.
All dharmas join together
to make life possible.

The kitchen can be a meditative practice space. Let us be mindful when we are cooking or cleaning. We can do our tasks in a relaxed and serene way, following our breathing and keeping our concentration on the work.

Practice

In your own kitchen, you might want to create a kitchen altar to remind yourself to practice mindfulness while cooking. It can be just a small shelf with enough room for an incense holder and perhaps a small flower vase, a beautiful stone, a small picture of an ancestor or a spiritual teacher, or a statue of the Buddha or a bodhisattva—what-ever is most meaningful to you. When you come into the kitchen, you can begin your work by offering incense and practicing mindful breathing, making the kitchen into a meditation hall.

While cooking, allow enough time so you don't feel rushed. Be aware that you, and anyone else you're cooking for, depend on this food for their practice. This awareness will guide you to cook healthy food infused with your love and mindfulness.

When you're cleaning the kitchen or washing dishes, do it as if you're cleaning the altar in the meditation hall or washing the baby Buddha. Washing in this way, you can feel joy and peace radiate within and around you.

Washing the dishes
is like bathing a baby Buddha.
The profane is the sacred.
Everyday mind is Buddha's mind.

TEA MEDITATION

Tea meditation is a time to be with our community in a joyful and serene atmosphere. Just to enjoy our tea together is enough. It is like a "good news" occasion, when we share our joy and happiness in being together.

At times, when we are drinking tea with a friend, we are not aware of the tea or even of our friend sitting there. Practicing tea meditation is to be truly present with our tea and our friends. We recognize that we can dwell happily in the present moment despite all of our sorrows and worries. We sit there relaxed without having to say anything. If we like, we may also share a song, a story, or a dance.

We may like to bring a musical instrument or prepare something ahead of time. It is an opportunity for us to water the seeds of happiness and joy, of understanding and love in each one of us.

Practice

Here is the way we organize a formal tea meditation in Plum Village. Children enjoy this practice very much. They can help greet the guests as they enter, and a child can be the one to offer the tea and cookie to the Buddha. Sometimes the children organize their own lemonade meditation to which they invite their parents and friends. You can modify the tea ceremony to fit any occasion. Tea meditation can be as simple as sharing a cup of tea with a good friend.

In a Tea Ceremony, everything is done with mindfulness. The hosts for the Tea Ceremony will need to come together as a team well in advance. They will need to prepare the tea and biscuits, the meditation room, and themselves in mindfulness in order to welcome their honored guests.

HOSTS

Tea Master, Bell Master, Incense Offerer, Tea Offerer (who offers tea to the Buddha), Tea Servers (depending on numbers, usually two are needed), Assistant Tea Servers (one for each Tea Server)

ITEMS NEEDED

Incense, candles, matches, small bell, large bell, napkins (leaves can be used), cookies, tea and teapots, trays, plate with flower, tea and cookie for offering to the Buddha

WELCOMING THE GUESTS

- The hosts for the tea meditation stand in two rows on each side of the entry door and bow to each guest as they enter the meditation room. The guests pass between the hosts and sit in sequence around the room facing inward, ushered to their cushions by the Tea Assistants. While seated, everyone enjoys sitting meditation, following their breath in silence.
- Once everyone has been welcomed into the room, the hosts take their seats. The Bell Master wakes up and invites the small bell to signal to

people to stand up and face the altar.

INCENSE OFFERING

- The Tea Master and the Incense Offerer walk mindfully to the altar, and the Incense Offerer lights incense. After bowing to each other, the Incense Offerer passes the incense to the Tea Master and stands to the side.
- The Bell Master invites the large bell three times. The Tea Master chants the incense offering before passing incense to the Incense Offerer who places it at the altar. This is the time when, if we wish, we can bow to the Buddha and bodhisattvas.[4]
- The Tea Master turns to face the community and welcomes everyone to the Tea Ceremony. "A lotus for you, all buddhas to be!" The Bell Master invites the small bell, and everyone sits down.

---

[4] See Thich Nhat Hanh, Chanting From the Heart (Berkeley, CA: Parallax Press, 2007) p.28.

OFFERING FOR THE BUDDHA

- A Tea Server mindfully pours tea into a cup to offer to the Buddha and holds the decorated plate/tray with tea and cookie for offering at head level. The Tea Offerer walks mindfully to the Tea Server, bows, takes the plate, and walks mindfully to the Tea Master. The Tea Master stands up, bows, takes the Buddha's plate, and walks mindfully to the altar, bows, kneels, and places the plate on the altar. The Bell Master invites the bell as the plate is placed on the altar. The Tea Offerer and Tea Master return to their cushions and bow to each other before sitting down. If a child or a young person is present, they can be the one to place the offering on the altar.

SERVING THE GUESTS

- The Tea Servers now pass the tray of cookies. A Tea Server offers the cookie tray to an assistant. Smiling and offering a lotus in gratitude, the

assistant mindfully takes a cookie and napkin, places them on the floor, then takes the tray. The assistant now offers a cookie back to the Tea Server. The tray is then offered to the person sitting next to the assistant. As described above, each person takes a cookie and napkin before taking the tray and offering it to the next person in the circle.
- While the biscuits are passed, the Tea Servers pour the tea (filling as many cups as there are people present). When the trays for cookies are returned, the trays with teacups are passed around the circle and received just like the cookies. A small jug of milk and a sugar bowl can be present for people who like milk and/or sugar in their tea.

INVITATION TO SHARE

- Once the empty trays are returned, the Tea Master offers a gatha on enjoying tea and cookies and invites everyone to enjoy their tea and cookie.

TEA GATHA

This cup of tea in my two hands,
Mindfulness is held uprightly.
My body and mind dwell
In the very here and now.

After enjoying tea in silence for a short while, the Tea Master invites people to share songs, poems, experiences, etc.

ENDING THE CEREMONY

The Bell Master should announce when there are five minutes left before the end of the ceremony. The Tea Ceremony ends with three small bells. At the first, everyone stands up. At the second, they bow to each other. At the third, they bow to the altar. The hosts then go to the door first and bow to guests as they leave slowly and mindfully.

PHYSICAL PRACTICES

RESTING AND STOPPING

When a forest animal is sick, it lies down and does nothing. Often it won't even eat or drink. All of its energy is directed toward healing. We need to practice this kind of resting even when we are not sick. Knowing when to rest is a deep practice. Sometimes we try too hard in our practice or we work too much without mindfulness, and we become tired very easily. The practice of mindfulness should not be tiring, rather it should be energizing. But when we recognize that we are tired, we should find every means possible to rest. We need to ask for help, delegating tasks whenever possible.

Practicing with a tired body and mind doesn't help; it can cause more problems. To take care of ourselves is to take care of our whole community. Resting may mean we stop what we're doing and take a five-minute walk outside, or we go on a fast for a day or two, or it may mean we practice silence for a period. There are many ways for us to rest, so we must pay attention to the rhythm of our bodies and minds for the benefit of all. Mindful breathing, whether in the sitting or in the lying position, is the practice of resting. Let us learn the art of resting and allow our body and our mind to restore themselves. Not thinking and not doing anything is part of the art of resting and healing.

The Buddha said that if we have a wound within our body or within our mind, we can learn how to take care of it. We know that our body has the capacity to heal itself, so we should allow the wound in our body and soul to heal. But very often we stand in the way of its healing. Because of our ignorance, we forbid our body to heal itself; we don't allow our mind, our consciousness, to heal itself. When we cut our finger, we don't have to do much. We just clean the cut and allow it to heal—maybe for one or two days. If we tamper with the wound, if we do too many things to it or worry too much about it—especially if we worry too much—it may not heal.

The Buddha gave the example of someone who is hit by an arrow. The person suffers. If, soon afterward, a second arrow strikes him in exactly the same spot, the pain is not just double but ten times more intense. If you have a small wound within your body and you magnify it with your worry and your panic, the wound will become more serious. It would be helpful to practice breathing in and breathing out and understanding the nature of the little wound. Breathing in, we think, "I am aware that this is only a physical wound. It will heal." If we need to, we can ask a friend or a doctor to confirm that our wound is only minor, and that we shouldn't worry. We shouldn't panic, because panic is born from ignorance. Worry and panic make any situation worse. We should rely on our knowledge of our own body. We are intelligent. We shouldn't imagine that we are going to die because of a minor wound in our body or soul.

A wounded animal knows that rest is the best way to heal. Wisdom is present in the animal's body. We human beings have lost confidence in our body.

We panic and try to do many different things. We worry too much about our body. We don't allow it to heal itself. We don't know how to rest. Mindful breathing helps us to relearn the art of resting. Mindful breathing is like a loving mother holding her sick baby in her arms, saying, "Don't worry, I'll take good care of you; just rest."

Practice

If we can't rest, it's because we haven't stopped running. We began running a long time ago. We continue to run even in our sleep. We think that happiness and well-being are not possible in the here and the now. That belief is inherent in us. We received the seed of that belief from our parents and our grandparents. They struggled all of their lives and believed that happiness was only possible in the future. That's why when we were children, we were already in the habit of running. We believed that happiness was something to seek for in the future. But the teaching of the Buddha is that we can be happy right here, right now.

If you can stop and establish yourself in the here and the now, you will see that there are many elements of happiness available in this moment, more than enough for you to be happy. Even if there are a few things in the present that you dislike, there are still plenty of positive conditions for your happiness. When you walk in the garden, you may see that a tree is dying. You may feel sorry about that and may not be able to enjoy the rest of the garden that is still beautiful. You allow one dying tree to destroy your appreciation of all the other trees that are still alive, vigorous, and beautiful. If you look again, you can see that the garden is still beautiful, and you can enjoy it. You can use these verses to heighten your awareness of the nature around you:

Aware of my ears, I breathe in.
Aware of the sound of rain, I breathe out.

In touch with pure mountain air, I breathe in.
Smiling with pure mountain air, I breathe out.

*In touch with the sunshine, I breathe in.
Smiling with the sunshine, I breathe out.*

*In touch with the trees, I breathe in.
Smiling with the trees, I breathe out.*

DEEP RELAXATION

Stress accumulates in our body. The way we eat, drink, and live takes its toll on our well-being. Deep relaxation is an opportunity for our body to rest, heal, and be restored. We relax our body, give our attention to each part in turn, and send our love and care to every cell.

If you have trouble sleeping enough, deep relaxation can compensate. Lying awake on your bed, you may like to practice total relaxation and follow your breathing in and breathing out. Sometimes this can help you get to sleep. The practice is still very good even if you don't sleep, because it nourishes you and allows you to rest.

You can use these two exercises to guide awareness to any part of the body: the hair, scalp, brain, ears, neck, lungs, each of the internal organs, the digestive system, pelvis; any part of the body that needs healing and attention, embracing each part and sending love, gratitude, and care as we hold it in our awareness and breathe in and out.

Practice

DEEP RELAXATION I

If you only have a few minutes to sit or lie down and relax, you can recite this verse:

Breathing in, I am aware of my eyes.
Breathing out, I smile to my eyes.

This is mindfulness of our eyes. When you generate the energy of mindfulness, you embrace your eyes and smile to them. You touch one of the conditions for happiness that exists. Having eyes that are still in good condition is a wonderful thing. A paradise of forms and colors is available to you at any time. You need only to open your eyes.

Breathing in, I am aware of my heart.
Breathing out, I smile to my heart.

When you use the energy of mindfulness to embrace your heart and smile to it, you see that your heart is still functioning normally, and that is a wonderful thing. Many people wish they had a heart that functioned normally. It is the basic condition for our well-being, another condition for our happiness. When you hold your heart with the energy of mindfulness, your heart is comforted. You have neglected your heart for a long time. You think only of other things. You run after things that you believe to be the true conditions for happiness while you forget your heart.

You even cause trouble for your heart in the way you rest, work, eat, and drink. Every time you light a cigarette, you make your heart suffer. You commit an unfriendly act toward your heart when you drink alcohol. You know that your heart has been working for your well-being for many years, day and night. But because of your lack of mindfulness, you have not been very helpful to your heart. You do not know how to protect the conditions of well-being and happiness within you.

You can continue to do this practice with other parts of your body, like your liver. Embrace your liver with tenderness, love, and compassion. Generate mindfulness by means of mindful breathing and hold your body in mindfulness. When you direct the energy of mindfulness to the part of your body that you are embracing with love and tenderness, you are doing exactly what your body needs. If a part of your body doesn't feel well, you have to spend more time holding it with mindfulness, with your smile. You may not have time to follow your whole body in this exercise, but once or twice each day you can pick at least one part of your body to focus on and practice relaxing. If you have more time, try the second deep relaxation practice below.

Practice

DEEP RELAXATION II

Give yourself at least twenty minutes. When you do deep relaxation in a group, one person can guide the exercise using the following cues or some variation of them. When you do deep relaxation on your own, you may like to record an exercise to follow as you practice. Deep relaxation can be done at home at least once a day, wherever you have the space to lie comfortably. You can do it with others in your family, with one member leading the session.

Lie down on your back with your arms at your sides. Make yourself comfortable. Allow your body to relax. Be aware of the floor beneath you ... and of the contact of your body with the floor. (Breathe.) Allow your body to sink into the floor. (Breathe.)

Become aware of your breathing, in and out. Be aware of your abdomen rising and falling as you breathe in and out. (Breathe.) Rising ... falling ... rising ... falling. (Breathe.)

Breathing in, bring your awareness to your eyes. Breathing out, allow your eyes to relax. Allow your eyes to sink back into your head ... let go of the tension in all the tiny muscles around your eyes...our eyes allow us to see a paradise of form and color ... allow your eyes to rest ... send love and gratitude to your eyes.... (Breathe.)

Breathing in, bring your awareness to your mouth. Breathing out, allow your mouth to relax. Release the tension around your mouth ... your lips are the petals of a flower ... let a gentle smile bloom on your lips ... smiling releases the tension in the hundreds of muscles in your face ... feel the tension release in your cheeks ... your jaw ... your throat.... (Breathe.)

Breathing in, bring your awareness to your shoulders. Breathing out, allow your shoulders to relax. Let them sink into the floor ... let all the accumulated tension flow into the floor ... you carry so much with your shoulders ... now let them relax as you care for your shoulders. (Breathe.)

Breathing in, become aware of your arms. Breathing out, relax your arms. Let your arms sink into the floor ... your upper arms ... your elbows ... your lower arms ... your wrists ... hands ... fingers ... all the tiny muscles ... move your fingers a little if you need to, to help the muscles relax. (Breathe.)

Breathing in, bring your awareness to your heart. Breathing out, allow your heart to relax. (Breathe.) You have neglected your heart for a long time ... by the way you work, eat, and manage anxiety and stress.... (Breathe.) Your heart beats for you night and day ... embrace your heart with mindfulness and tenderness ... reconciling and taking care of your heart. (Breathe.)

Breathing in, bring your awareness to your legs. Breathing out, allow your legs to relax. Release all the tension in your legs ... your thighs ... your knees ... your calves ... your ankles ... your feet ... your toes ... all the tiny muscles in your toes ... you may want to move your toes a little to help them relax ... send your love and care to your toes. (Breathe.)

Breathing in, breathing out ... your whole body feels light ... like duck-weed floating on the water ... you have nowhere to go ... nothing to do ... you are free as the cloud floating in the sky.... (Breathe.)

(Singing or music for some minutes.) (Breathe.)

Bring your awareness back to your breathing ... to your abdomen rising and falling. (Breathe.)

Following your breathing, become aware of your arms and legs ... you may want to move them a little and stretch. (Breathe.)

When you feel ready, slowly sit up. (Breathe.)

When you are ready, slowly stand up.

MINDFUL MOVEMENTS

The Ten Mindful Movement exercises are easy to do at home, by yourself, or with others. You can do them inside your home or outside in the park. You can do them every day or just once in a while.

Practice

Stand with your feet firmly on the ground. Your knees are soft, slightly bent and not locked. Stand upright in a relaxed way, with your shoulders loose. Imagine an invisible thread is attached to the top of your head and it pulls you up toward the sky. Keeping your body straight, tuck your chin in slightly so your neck can relax.

Begin by practicing a little bit of conscious breathing. Make sure your feet are placed firmly on the earth, your body is centered, your back is straight, and your shoulders are relaxed. Allow your breathing to come down into your belly. You may like to smile and enjoy standing for just one moment.

MINDFUL MOVEMENT ONE Begin with your feet slightly apart, arms at your sides. Breathing in, keep your elbows straight as you lift your arms in front of you until they're shoulder level, horizontal to the ground. Breathing out, bring your arms down again to your sides. Repeat the movement three more times.

MINDFUL MOVEMENT TWO Begin with your arms at your sides. Breathing in, lift your arms in front of you in one continuous movement, bringing them all the way up and stretching them above your head. Touch the sky! This movement can be done with your palms either facing inward toward each other, or facing forward as you reach up. Breathing out, bring your arms slowly down again to your sides. Repeat three more times.

MINDFUL MOVEMENT THREE Breathing in, lift your arms out to the side, palms up, until your arms are shoulder level, parallel to the ground. Breathing out, bend your elbows and touch your shoulders with your fingertips, keeping your upper arms horizontal. Breathing in, open your arms, extending them until they're stretched out to a horizontal position again. Breathing out, bend your elbows, bringing your fingertips back to your shoulders. When you breathe in, you're like a flower opening to the warm sun. Breathing out, the flower closes. From this position with your fingertips on your shoulders, do the movement three more times. Then lower your arms back down to your sides.

MINDFUL MOVEMENT FOUR In this exercise, you make a large circle with your arms. Breathing in, bring your arms straight down in front of you with your palms together. Raise your arms up and separate your hands so your arms can stretch up over your head. Breathing out, continue the circle, with your arms circling back, until your fingers point down toward the ground. Breathing in, lift your arms up behind you and reverse the circle. Breathe out as you bring your palms together and your arms come down in front of you. Repeat three more times.

MINDFUL MOVEMENT FIVE Adjust your feet so they're shoulder-width apart and put your hands on your waist. As you do this exercise, keep your legs straight but not locked, and your head centered over your body. Breathing in, bend forward at the waist and begin to make a circle to the back with your upper body. When you're halfway through the circle, your upper body leaning back, breathe out while you complete the circle, ending with your head in front of you while you're still bent at the waist. Then circle, in the same way, in the other direction. Repeat the series of movements three more times.

MINDFUL MOVEMENT SIX This exercise is called the frog. Begin with your hands on your waist, heels together, feet turned out to form a V, so that they make a ninety-degree angle. Breathing in, rise up on your toes, keep your back straight, and bend your knees. Keeping your upper body centered, go down as low as you comfortably can, maintaining your balance. Breathing in, straighten your knees and come all the way up, still standing on your toes. From this position, repeat the movement three more times, remembering to breathe slowly and deeply.

MINDFUL MOVEMENT SEVEN In this exercise, you touch the sky and the earth. Stand with your feet hip-width apart. Breathing in, bring your arms up above your head, palms forward. Stretch all the way up and look up as you touch the sky. Breathing out, bend at the waist as you bring your arms down to touch the earth. If there is tension in your neck, let it go. From this position, breathe in and keep your back straight as you come all the way back up and touch the sky. Touch the earth and sky three more times.

MINDFUL MOVEMENT EIGHT Start with your feet together and your hands on your waist. Begin by putting all your weight on your left foot. Breathing in, lift your right thigh as you bend your knee and keep your toes pointed toward the ground. Breathing out, stretch your right leg out in front of you, keeping your toes pointed. Breathing in, bend your knee and bring your foot back toward your body. Breathing out, put your right foot back on the ground. Next put all your weight onto your right foot and do the movement with the other leg. Repeat the series of movements three more times.

MINDFUL MOVEMENT NINE In this exercise, you make a circle with your leg. Begin with your feet together and your hands on your waist. Put your weight on your left foot and, breathing in, lift your right leg in front of you and circle it to the side. Breathing out, continue the circle to the back and bring your leg down behind you, allowing your toes to touch the ground. Breathing in, lift your leg up behind you and circle it to the side. Breathing out, continue the circle to the front. Then lower your leg and put your foot on the ground, allowing your weight to again be on both feet. Stand feet together, weight on both feet. Now do the exercise with the other leg. Repeat the series of movements three more times.

Mindful Movement Ten: This exercise is done in a lunge position. Stand with your feet slightly wider than shoulder-width apart. Turn to the right and put your right foot out in front of you so you are in a lunge. Put your left hand on your waist and your right arm at your side. Breathing in, bend your right knee, bringing your weight over your right foot as you lift your right arm with the palm of your hand facing outward in front of you, and stretch it to the sky! Breathe out, straightening your knee and bringing your right arm back to your side. Repeat the movement three more times.

Switch legs, putting your right hand on your waist. Repeat the movement on the left four times. Then bring your feet back together again.

You have finished the Ten Mindful Movements. Stand firmly on two feet and breathe in and out. Feel your body relax. Enjoy your breathing.

RELATIONSHIP & COMMUNITY PRACTICES

CREATING AND MAINTAINING A SANGHA

In society, much of our suffering comes from feeling disconnected from one another. We often don't feel a real connection even with people we live close to, our neighbors, our coworkers, and even our family members. Each person lives separately, cut off from the support of the community.

Practicing mindfulness, we begin to see our connection with other human beings. To flourish in our own practice and to support others, we need a community. In Buddhism, a practice community is called a *Sangha.* The Buddha had a Sangha of monks, nuns, lay-women, and laymen. We can make our families into a Sangha. We can make our workplace into a Sangha, our neighborhood into a Sangha, local government into a Sangha, and even the Congress could turn into a Sangha if everyone knew the art of deep listening and loving speech.

Being with a Sangha can heal these feelings of isolation and separation. We practice together, sometimes we eat side by side and clean pots together. Just by participating with other practitioners in daily activities, we can experience a tangible feeling of love and acceptance.

The Sangha is a garden, full of many varieties of trees and flowers. When we can look at ourselves and at others as beautiful, unique flowers and trees we can truly grow to understand and love one another. One flower may bloom early in the spring and another flower may bloom in late summer. One tree may bear many fruits and another tree may offer cool shade. No one plant is greater or lesser or the same as any other plant in the garden. Each member of the Sangha also has unique gifts to offer to the community. We each have areas that need attention as well. When we can appreciate each member's contribution and see our weaknesses as potential for growth, we can learn to live together harmoniously. Our practice is to see that we are a flower or a tree, and we are the whole garden as well, all interconnected.

To be really means to inter-be. Just as a flower relies on the sunshine, on the cloud, on the earth in order to be, so it is with all of us. None of us can be by ourselves alone. Interbeing is the teaching of the Buddha that everything is made by and made up of everything else. If we return everything to its source, there's nothing left any-more. If we return the sunshine to the sun, the water to the cloud, the soil to the earth, then there can no longer be any flower. A flower is made only of non-flower elements. That is why we say a flower is empty of self; it's empty of a separate self. It's full of everything and empty of a separate self. We are empty, and we are made of the cosmos. Looking at one person, we can see the whole cosmos and all our ancestors. In each person, we can see the air, water, journeys, joys, and sorrows that have come before us. We contain all information needed for the understanding of the cosmos. If we can see the nature of interbeing, then we will suffer much less and we will understand why it is important to be in community.

In practicing together as a community, our practice of mindfulness becomes more joyful, relaxed, and steady. We are bells of mindfulness for each other, supporting and reminding each other along the path of practice. With the support of the community, we can practice to cultivate peace and joy within and around us, as a gift for all of those whom we love and care for. We can cultivate our solidity and freedom—solid in our deepest aspiration and free from our fears, misunderstandings, and suffering.

Practice

Building a Sangha is like planting a sunflower. You need to be aware of which conditions will support the flower's growth and which conditions will obstruct its growth. You need healthy seeds, skilled gardeners, and plenty of sunshine and room to grow. When you engage in Sangha building, the most important thing to remember is that we are doing it together. The more you embrace the Sangha, the more you can let go of the feeling of a separate self. You can relax into the collective wisdom and insights of the Sangha and see clearly that the Sangha eyes and hands and heart are greater than that of any individual member of the Sangha.

If you live with your family or with close friends, this is a good place to begin. Your family and friends can be your Sangha. You can also create a "workplace Sangha" by practicing love and understanding with coworkers and seeing each person as a beloved brother or sister. You can practice walking meditation every time you move through a corridor.

If possible, sit, walk, or eat mindfully together with one other person during your breaks. You can invite the bell and invite others to do so with you, or practice telephone meditation at work. A Sangha may start small; it can be a Sangha of two. If even just two people create a Sangha and an atmosphere of mindfulness, the peace and harmony around you will grow and soon your Sangha will grow too.

BEGINNING ANEW

To begin anew is to look deeply and honestly at ourselves, our past actions, speech, and thoughts and to create a fresh beginning within ourselves and in our relationships with others. We practice Beginning Anew to clear our mind and keep our practice fresh. When a difficulty arises in our relationships and one of us feels resentment or hurt, we know it is time to begin anew.

Beginning Anew helps us develop our kind speech and compassionate listening because it is a practice of recognition and appreciation of the positive elements within our Sangha. Recognizing others' positive traits allows us to see our own good qualities as well. Along with these good traits, we each have areas of weakness, such as talking out of our anger or being caught in our misperceptions. As in a garden, when we "water the flowers" of loving kindness and compassion in each other, we also take energy away from the weeds of anger, jealousy, and misperception.

We can practice Beginning Anew everyday by expressing our appreciation to the people in our community and apologizing right away when we do or say something that hurts them. We can politely let others know when we have been hurt as well. The health and happiness of the whole community depends on the harmony, peace, and joy that exist between everyone.

Practice

At Plum Village we practice Beginning Anew every week. Everyone sits in a circle with a vase of fresh flowers in the center, and we follow our breathing as we wait for the facilitator to begin. The ceremony has three parts: flower watering, expressing regrets, and expressing hurts and difficulties. This practice can prevent feelings of hurt from building up over the weeks and helps make the situation safe for everyone in the community.

We begin with flower watering. When someone is ready to speak, she joins her palms and the others join their palms to show that she has the right to speak. Then she stands, walks slowly to the flowers, takes the vase in her hands, and returns to her seat. When she speaks, her words reflect the freshness and beauty of the flowers that are in her hands. During flower watering, the speaker acknowledges the wholesome, wonderful qualities of the others. It is not flattery; we always speak the truth. Everyone has strong points that can be seen with awareness. No one can interrupt the person holding the flowers. She is allowed as much time as she needs, and everyone else practices deep listening. When she has finished speaking, she stands up and slowly returns the vase to the center of the room.

We should not underestimate the first step of flower watering. When we can sincerely recognize the beautiful qualities of other people, it is very difficult to hold onto our feelings of anger and resentment. We will naturally soften and our perspective will become wider and more inclusive of the whole reality. When we are no longer caught in misperceptions, irritation, and judgment, we can easily find the way to reconcile ourselves with others in our community or family. The essence of this practice is to restore love and understanding between members of the community. The form that the practice takes needs to be appropriate to the situation and people involved. It is always helpful to consult with others who have more experience in the practice and have gone through similar difficulties in order to benefit from their experiences.

In the second part of the ceremony, we express regrets for anything we have done to hurt others. It does not take more than one thoughtless phrase to hurt someone. The ceremony of Beginning Anew is an opportunity for us to recall some regret from earlier in the week and undo it.

In the third part of the ceremony, we express ways in which others have hurt us. Loving speech is crucial. We want to heal the community, not harm it. We speak frankly, but we do not want to be destructive. Listening meditation is an important part of the practice. When we sit among a circle of friends who are all practicing deep listening, our speech becomes more beautiful and more constructive. We never blame or argue.

In this final part of the ceremony, compassionate listening is crucial. We listen to another's hurts and difficulties with the willingness to relieve the suffering of the other person, not to judge or argue with her. We listen with all our attention. Even if we hear something that is not true, we continue to listen deeply so the other person can express her pain and release the tensions within herself. If we reply to her or correct her, the practice will not bear fruit. We just listen. If we need to tell the other person that her perception was not correct, we can do that a few days later, privately and calmly. Then, at the next Beginning Anew session, she may be the person who rectifies the error, and we will not have to say anything. We close the ceremony with a song or by holding hands with everyone in the circle and breathing for a minute.

PEACE TREATY

Suppose our friend or partner says something unkind to us, and we feel hurt. If we reply right away, we risk making the situation worse. Another option is to breathe in and out to calm ourselves, and when we are calm enough, say, "Darling, what you just said hurt me. I would like to look deeply into it, and I would like you to look deeply into it, also. Then we can make an appointment for some time later in the week to look at it together." One person looking at the roots of our suffering is good, two people looking at it is better, and two people looking together is best.

We may be at war with ourselves inside, hurting our bodies with drugs or alcohol. Now we have the opportunity to sign a treaty with our bodies, our feelings, and our emotions. Once we make a peace treaty with them, we can have some peace, and we can begin to be reconciled with our beloved. If there is a war inside us, it is very easy to start a war with our beloved, not to mention with our enemies. The way we talk to our loved ones and the way we act toward them determines if we are treating them as loved ones or as enemies. If our beloved is our enemy, how can we hope to have peace in this country and in the world?

We all have the seed of wisdom in us. We know that punishing leads us nowhere, and yet we are always trying to punish someone. When our beloved says or does something that makes us suffer, we want to punish them, because we believe that by punishing them we will get some relief. There are times when we are lucid and we know that this is childish and ignorant, because when we make our beloved ones suffer, they will also try to get some relief by punishing us in turn, and there will be an escalation of punishment.

The Peace Treaty and the Peace Note are two tools to help us heal anger and hurt in our relationships. When we sign the Peace Treaty, we are making peace not just with the other person, but within ourselves.

Practice

The text of the Peace Treaty is below. It helps to really sign it, as opposed to just reading about it. In the treaty, it suggests Friday night as the night for discussion. You can pick any night, but the treaty suggests Friday evening is good for two reasons. If it's Friday afternoon when you begin, you can pick the following Friday. First, you are still hurt, and it may be too risky if you begin discussing it now. You might say things that will make the situation worse. From now until Friday evening, you can practice looking deeply into the nature of your suffering, and the other person can too. While driving, you will also have a chance to look deeply into it. Before Friday night, one or both of you may see the root of the problem and be able to tell the other and apologize. Then on Friday night, you can have a cup of tea together and enjoy each other. This is the practice of meditation. Meditation is to calm ourselves and to look deeply into the nature of our suffering.

If by Friday evening the suffering has not been transformed, you will be able to practice the art of Avalokiteshvara: one person expressing himself, while the other person listens deeply. When you speak, you tell the deepest kind of truth using loving speech, the kind of speech the other person can understand and accept. While listening, you know that your listening must be of a good quality to relieve the other person of his suffering. The second reason for waiting until Friday is that when you neutralize that feeling on Friday evening, you have Saturday and Sunday to enjoy being together.

PEACE TREATY

In order that we may live long and happily together, in order that we may continually develop and deepen our love and understanding, we the under-signed vow to observe and practice the following:

I, the one who is angry, agree to:

1. Refrain from saying or doing anything that might cause further damage or escalate the anger.
2. Not suppress my anger.
3. Practice breathing and taking refuge in the island of myself.
4. Calmly, within twenty-four hours, tell the one who has made me angry about my anger and suffering, either verbally or by delivering a Peace Note.
5. Ask for an appointment for later in the week (e.g., Friday evening) to discuss this matter more thoroughly, either verbally or by Peace Note.
6. Not say: "I am not angry. It's okay. I am not suffering. There is nothing to be angry about, at least not enough to make me angry."
7. Practice breathing and looking deeply into my daily life—while sitting, lying down, standing, and walking—in order to see:
    a. the ways I myself have been unskillful at times.
    b. how I have hurt the other person because of my own habit energy.

       c. how the strong seed of anger in me is the primary cause of my anger.
       d. how the other person's suffering, which waters the seed of my anger, is the secondary cause.
       e. how the other person is only seeking relief from his or her own suffering.
       f. that as long as the other person suffers, I cannot be truly happy.
8. Apologize immediately, without waiting until the Friday evening, as soon as I realize my unskillfulness and lack of mindfulness.
9. Postpone the Friday meeting if I do not feel calm enough to meet with the other person.

I, the one who has made the other angry, agree to:
1. Respect the other person's feelings, not ridicule him or her, and allow enough time for him or her to calm down.
2. Not press for an immediate discussion.
3. Confirm the other person's request for a meeting, either verbally or by

note, and assure him or her that I will be there.
4. Practice breathing and taking refuge in the island of myself to see how:
   a. I have seeds of unkindness and anger as well as the habit energy to make the other person unhappy.
   b. I have mistakenly thought that making the other person suffer would relieve my own suffering.
   c. by making him or her suffer, I make myself suffer.
5. Apologize as soon as I realize my unskillfulness and lack of mindfulness, without making any attempt to justify myself and without waiting until the Friday meeting.

We vow, with Lord Buddha as witness and the mindful presence of the sangha, to abide by these articles and to practice wholeheartedly. We invoke the three gems for protection and to grant us clarity and confidence.

Signed,
the _____ Day of _____
in the Year _____ in _____.

Practice

This note can be used with the Peace Treaty. You can copy it and keep blank copies available in your home and wherever you need it.

PEACE NOTE

Date:
Time:
Dear _____
This morning (afternoon), you said (did) something that made me very angry. I suffered very much. I want you to know this. You said (did):
Please let us both look at what you said (did) and examine the matter together in a calm and open manner this Friday evening.
Yours, not very happy right now, _____

SECOND BODY SYSTEM

In a large community or even a large family, it isn't possible to always be aware of what is going on with everyone. So in Plum Village we have developed something called the Second Body system to help build our Sangha. Your own body is your First Body, and someone else in your family or Sangha is your Second Body. Your Second Body picks someone else to be her Second Body and so on until you make a circle. In this way, everyone has someone to look after, and everyone is looked after by someone else.

Looking after means taking care of and helping our Second Body when she is physically ill, afflicted in mind, or overworked. For example, when we are traveling together, we are responsible to see that our Second Body is not left behind. When our Second Body's spirits are low, we can find a way to raise them. When our Second Body is not able to smile, we can help her to smile.

When she has the flu, we can bring her food and medicine. We use the Second Body system in all the Plum Village practice centers, and it raises the quality of our happiness in living together. It can be a wonderful way to stay connected to the whole community by taking care of just one member. In large families, it works the same.

Practice

Your First Body is your self. Your Second Body is another person who you look after as an extension of yourself. If you are my Second Body, then I am your Caring Friend. Everyone chooses one person to be his Second Body, and that person chooses someone else; so we create a complete circle with each person linked to the next. You should feel very connected to your Second Body, as if he is a part of yourself that we want to pay attention to and care for. So if your Second Body is not well, you find out how you can assist him, such as bringing meals to his room and letting the community know that your second body is ill. If you notice that your Second Body is less than happy, by asking and observing you may see a way that you can help. If you need to miss an activity, let your Caring Friend know.

Your Caring Friend is not a police officer keeping watch over your activities, rather he is someone who shows special care and concern for you, and you in turn show special care for your Second Body. Remember that each person has somewhat different needs, so be sensitive and intelligent in how you show your care. Sometimes, a few words of kindness are needed, and at other times, dwelling in your own island of conscious breathing is the best support for your friend.

Caring for our Second Body is a very concrete practice for us to stay connected to each other and to realize how we are all truly parts of one body. Everyone in the Sangha has his Second Body. Thus, the person whom your Second Body is taking care of is your Third Body. Therefore, by taking care of your Second Body you are taking care of the whole community.

HUGGING MEDITATION

When we hug, our hearts connect and we know that we are not separate beings. Hugging with mindfulness and concentration can bring reconciliation, healing, understanding, and much happiness. The practice of mindful hugging has helped so many to reconcile with each other—fathers and sons, mothers and daughters, friends and friends, and so many others.

Practice

You may practice hugging meditation with a friend, your daughter, your father, your partner, or even with a tree. To practice, first bow and recognize the presence of the other. Close your eyes, take a deep breath, and visualize yourself and your beloved three hundred years from now. Then you can enjoy three deep conscious breaths to bring ourselves fully there. Practice breathing in and breathing out to bring your insight of impermanence to life. "Breathing in, I know that life is precious in this moment. Breathing out, I cherish this moment of life." Smile at the person in front of you, expressing your desire to hold him or her in your arms. This is a practice and a ritual. When you bring your body and mind together to produce your total presence, to become full of life, it is a ritual.

When I drink a glass of water, I invest one hundred percent of myself in drinking it. You should train yourself to live every moment of your daily life like that. Hugging is a deep practice. You need to be totally present to do it correctly.

Then open your arms and begin hugging. Hold each other for three in- and out-breaths. With the first breath, you are aware that you are present in this very moment, and you are happy. With the second breath, you are aware that the other is present in this moment, and they are happy as well. With the third breath, you are aware that you are here together, right now on this Earth, and you feel deep gratitude and happiness for your togetherness. You then may release the other person and bow to each other to show your thanks.

You can also practice it in the following way: during the first in-breath and out-breath, become aware that you and your beloved are both alive; for the second in-breath and out-breath, think of where you will both be three hundred years from now; and for the third in-breath and out-breath, go back to the insight that you are both alive.

When you hug in such a way, the other person becomes real and alive. You do not need to wait until one of you is ready to depart for a trip, you may hug right now and receive the warmth and stability of your friend in the present moment. Hugging can be a deep practice of reconciliation.

During the silent hugging, the message can come out very clear: "Darling, you are precious to me. I am sorry I have not been mindful and considerate. I have made mistakes. Allow me to begin anew."

Life becomes real at that moment. Architects need to build airports and railway stations so that there is enough room to practice hugging. Your hugging will be deeper, and so will your happiness.

DEEP LISTENING AND LOVING SPEECH

When communication is cut off, we all suffer. When no one listens to us or understands us, we become like a bomb ready to explode. Compassionate listening brings about healing. Sometimes only ten minutes of listening deeply can transform us and bring a smile back to our lips.

Many of us have lost our capacity for listening and using loving speech in our families. It may be that no one is capable of listening to anyone else. So we feel very lonely even within our own families. We go to a therapist, hoping that she is able to listen to us. But many therapists also have deep suffering within. Sometimes they cannot listen as deeply as they would like. So if we really love someone, we need to train ourselves to be a deep listener.

We also need to train ourselves to use loving speech. We have lost our capacity to say things calmly. We get irritated too easily. Every time we open our mouths, our speech becomes sour or bitter. We have lost our capacity for speaking with kindness. Without this ability, we cannot succeed in restoring harmony, love, and happiness.

In Buddhism, we speak of bodhisattvas, wise and compassionate beings who stay on Earth to alleviate the suffering of others. The bodhisattva Avalokiteshvara, also called Quan Yin, is a person who has a great capacity for listening with compassion and true presence. Quan Yin is the bodhisattva who can listen and understand the sounds of the world, the cries of suffering.

Practice

You have to practice breathing mindfully in and out so that compassion always stays with you. You listen without giving advice or passing judgment. You can say to yourself about the other person, "I am listening to him just because I want to relieve his suffering." This is called compassionate listening. You have to listen in such a way that compassion remains with you the whole time you are listening. That is the art. If halfway through listening, irritation or anger comes up, then you cannot continue to listen. You have to practice in such a way that every time the energy of irritation and anger comes up, you can breathe in and out mindfully and continue to hold compassion within you. It is with compassion that you can listen to another. No matter what the other person says, even if there is a lot of strong information and injustice in his way of seeing things, even if he condemns or blames you, continue to sit very quietly breathing in and out.

If you don't feel that you can continue to listen in this way, let the other person know. Ask your friend, "Dear one, can we continue in a few days? I need to renew myself. I need to practice so that I can listen to you in the best way I can." If you are not in good shape, you are not going to listen in the best way you can. Practice more walking meditation, more mindful breathing, and more sitting meditation in order to restore your capacity for compassionate listening.

TAKING CARE OF ANGER AND OTHER STRONG EMOTIONS

Our anger is like a small child crying out for his mother. When the baby cries, the mother takes him gently in her arms and listens and observes carefully to find out what is wrong. The loving action of holding her baby with tenderness already soothes the baby's suffering. Likewise, we can take our anger in our loving arms and right away we will feel relief. We don't need to reject our anger. It is a part of us that needs our love and deep listening just as a baby does. After the baby has calmed down, the mother can feel if the baby has a fever or needs a change of diaper. When we feel calm and cool, we too can look deeply at our anger and see clearly the conditions allowing our anger to rise.

The book *Flowers in the Garden of Meditation* contains histories of different Zen masters. One master says, if a monk gets angry, he should not keep his anger over more than one night. In Vietnam children say, "Be angry, sad, or annoyed for five minutes." We have the right to be angry or sad, but five minutes is enough. The master of *Flowers in the Garden of Meditation* gives us the right to be angry all night, but the next morning our anger should have finished.

If we practice being present with our strong emotions, the energy of loving kindness and caring will reduce the anger or sorrow. Every time a storm arises, we know to return home and close all the windows and doors to prevent the rain and wind from entering our house and destroying it. If there is no electricity, we light up candles or oil lamps. If the weather is cold, we make a fire. We create an area of safety inside while the storms are happening outside.

A strong emotion is similar to a storm, and it can create a lot of damage. We need to figure out a way to protect ourselves, to create a safe environment, and to wait out the storm. We cannot sit and wait for the storm to go by quickly while we receive all the damage of the storm directly. Keeping our body and mind safe from the storm is our practice. After each storm, we become stronger, more solid, and soon we're no longer fearful of storms. We no longer pray for a calm sky and a calm ocean. Instead, we pray that we have the wisdom and strength to deal with the difficulties that arise in life.

We don't have to wait until the emotional storm arises in us to begin to practice. We have to practice today, and every day, for five to ten minutes. After a couple of weeks, we have a handle on our method of breathing, and when the emotional storms arise in us, we automatically remember to practice right away.

Practice

BEING WITH ANGER

When you feel angry, it's best to refrain from saying or doing anything. You may like to withdraw your attention from the person or situation, that is watering the seed of anger in you. Take this time to come back to yourself. Practice conscious breathing and outdoor walking meditation to calm and refresh your mind and body. After you feel calmer and more relaxed, you can begin to look deeply at yourself and at the person and situation causing anger to arise in you. Often, when you have a difficulty with a particular person, he may have a characteristic that reflects a weakness of your own which is difficult to accept. As you grow to love and accept yourself, this will naturally spread to those around you.

Walking meditation can be very helpful when you are angry. Try reciting this verse as you walk:

> *Breathing in, I know that anger is in me.*
> *Breathing out, I know this feeling is unpleasant.*

And then, after a while of walking meditation:

> *Breathing in, I feel calm.*
> *Breathing out, I am now strong enough to take care of this anger.*

Until you are calm enough to look directly at the anger, just enjoy your breathing, your walking, and the beauties of the outdoors. After a while, the anger will subside, and you will feel strong enough to look directly at it, to try to understand its causes, and to begin the work of transforming it.

If, when you are angry, you practice sitting meditation, you can meditate on this gatha:

> *Getting angry at each other in the ultimate dimension,*
> *we should only close our eyes and look into the future.*
> *In one hundred years from now, where will you be, and where shall I be?*

This is the insight of impermanence. When you get angry with the one you love, you want to punish him to get relief. That is a natural tendency. But if you just close your eyes and visualize yourself and your beloved one hundred or three hundred years from now, you will get the insight of impermanence. Just one in-breath and one out-breath is enough for you to get the insight.

When you open your eyes, you only want to do one thing, and that is to open your arms and hug that person. That is the only thing worth doing, to cherish his presence because of impermanence. It's only when you are unaware of the nature of impermanence that you get angry.

You suffer not because things are impermanent. You suffer because things are impermanent and you don't know that they are impermanent. This is very important. So, it is very helpful to practice mindful breathing in order to gain the insight of impermanence and keep it alive. Then you will know what to do and what not to do to make life more pleasant. Looking into a flower, looking into a cloud, looking into a living being, you touch the nature of impermanence. How important is impermanence? Without impermanence, nothing can be possible. Don't complain about impermanence. If things were not impermanent, how could a grain of corn become a corn plant? How could your child grow up? Impermanence is the ground of life. But although you live with the reality of impermanence every day, you deny it. When you practice looking deeply into things, you can discover the nature of impermanence, and make it a living insight that you carry with you in every minute of your life.

Practice

STRONG EMOTIONS I

Every time sadness or anger or disappointment surface, you have the capacity to deal with it. Because your anger, your disappointment, is part of you, don't fight against it or oppress it. To do so is to commit a violent act against yourself. Instead, each time a storm of strong emotion comes up, sit quietly, keep your back straight, return to your breath, return to your body, close all the windows of your senses.

You have six senses: eyes, ears, nose, tongue, body, and mind. Don't look, don't listen, and don't continue thinking about the thing that you believe is the source of your suffering: that one sentence, one letter, one action, or one piece of news. Return to yourself, take hold of your breathing, follow your breathing, hold tightly to your in-breath and out-breath, just like a captain holding tight to the wheel of a boat that is being tossed by the ocean waves. Mindful breathing is the anchor, the wheel, and the mast.

Breathe a long breath, paying complete attention to your breathing in and out. Pay attention to your lower belly, see that your belly contracts when you breathe out and expands when you're breathing in. Keep your attention at the level of your lower belly, don't let it wander in your head. Stop all thinking, only closely follow your breath. Remind yourself, "I have passed through many storms. Every storm has to pass, there is no storm that will stay there forever. This condition of the mind will also go by. Everything is impermanent. The storm is only a storm. We are not only a storm. We can find safety right in the storm. We will not let the storm create harm in us." When you can see it like that, when you remember it like that, you already begin to be your own boss, and you're no longer the victim of the emotional storm.

Looking at the top of a tree being tossed around by a storm, we have the feeling that the tree will be blown away by the storm at any moment. But if we look at the trunk and the base of the tree, we can see that the tree has many roots that attach deeply into the earth. We feel at ease, we know that the tree will stand strong. *Dantien* is the Vietnamese word for the energy point just below our belly button; it is the root of the tree. Pay attention to the lower part of your belly and don't let your thinking, seeing, or hearing pull you to the top of the tree. Practice breathing like that for five, ten, or fifteen minutes, keeping your mind focused only on your breathing and your lower belly, and let your emotions go by. When the storm of emotion passes, you know that you have the capacity to protect yourself, you have the ability to manage your emotional storms. You have faith in yourself, and you're no longer fearful. You have ways to protect yourself every time an emotional storm comes up or surfaces; therefore, you are very much at peace.

Practice

STRONG EMOTIONS II

If you're experiencing a difficult time in life, you'll need to bolster your feelings of happiness before you can work on your challenges. It might seem as if the reverse were true. But by nourishing yourself with happiness first, you lay the groundwork to address your pain.

The following meditation can help.

Sit still in a quiet spot and bring your awareness to your breath. Use the first of the following meditations to create a sense of inner joy. The second meditation will then give you the courage to address your feelings of pain.

1.

Breathing in, I am aware of the feeling of joy in myself.
Breathing out, I smile to the feeling of joy that is in myself.
Breathing in, I am aware of the feeling of happiness in myself.

Breathing out, I smile to the feeling of happiness that is in myself.

2.
Breathing in, I am aware of the painful feeling in me.
Breathing out, I release the tension within that painful feeling in me.

SHINING LIGHT

To shine light on a person means to use one's observation and insight in order to advise someone about his strengths and weaknesses in the practice and to propose ways to practice that he can profit from. This is an important practice that works best when there are deep relationships, regular practice, and strong connections between the people involved.

Practice

Each practitioner asks the Sangha to shine light upon her in order to help her to see herself more clearly, her strengths and weaknesses, and the quality of her practice. It is a very deep practice for those shining light as well as for the one receiving. It requires deep looking. We need to look at our brother and sister and get in touch with what we truly appreciate about his or her practice. The only motivation must be a desire to help that is generated from love and compassion for the person who is receiving.

The concerned person joins her palms and asks the Sangha to shine light on her: "Dear Sangha, please tell me of my strengths and weaknesses, and indicate to me the kind of practices I should take up in order to improve my practice." And then she will express herself concerning the practice she has taken up during the last few months: "Dear Sangha, I have these weaknesses, this kind of habit energy. I've been trying to become aware of these habit energies and have used these methods in order to overcome and transform my habit energies" and so on. "I've succeeded in these methods but haven't been very successful in transforming this and that." And the person will tell the Sangha how she sees herself.

Then each person in the Sangha takes a turn in order to tell her and the whole Sangha what he knows about that person. So everyone is listening, including the person who has asked the Sangha to shine light on her.

We do this practice only when we've lived together for at least three months;

it works quite well when the people have known each other for much longer than that. First, we water the flowers in the person on whom we're shining light. We tell her about her strengths, her goodness, and her positive aspects in order to help these things to grow. And then we talk about the things that could be improved, the weaknesses. This is always done with love, wisdom, and compassion. Because we are using loving speech, the person does not get hurt. Finally, we propose practices she can use to improve her temperament and so on. When we propose something, it should come from our own experiences. If we have practiced, if we have overcome difficulties, if we have transformed, we propose very concrete things that have helped us. What we say will be very close to the truth and will help that person to see herself more clearly, she will profit and will take up the things we suggest in order to improve her practice. We're not criticizing, but rather supporting and sharing in each person's path and practice.

It's important to have one person write down everything that has been said in the session of shining light. Another person will take the notes and put them into a letter called the letter of shining light. The letter of shining light has at least three parts. The first part of the letter talks about the positive points, the strengths, and the good qualities of the person. The second part of the letter deals with the weaknesses that are still there. And the third part of the letter is for making proposals as to how that person can improve his practice and quality of life. So there's a lot of love in the work of shining light on one person.

In the beginning, we may be very reluctant. We may be a little bit afraid that people will talk about our weaknesses; it sounds unpleasant. But soon we may find that we like it. We learn so much, we understand ourselves much better after a session of shining light.

If we sit in a session of shining light, we learn a lot. Everyone has his own vision. We combine everyone's vision into a collective vision, and we call it the Sangha eyes. Sangha eyes are always much brighter than the individual eyes. When we use our individual eyes to look, we may not see very clearly. But if thirty, forty, fifty people combine their observation, their vision, then that will bring us closer to the truth.

WRITING A LOVE LETTER

If we have difficulties with someone in our life, we might spend some time alone and write a letter to him. We can write the letter to someone we see every day or, just as effectively, to someone we have not seen for years. Many people have found this practice helpful when writing to a family member who is no longer living. To do the work of reconciliation is a great offering we can make to ourselves, our beloved ones, and our ancestors. We reconcile with our mother and father inside of us, and we might also discover a skillful way to reconcile with our mother and father outside of us. It is never too late to bring peace and healing into our blood family.

Practice

Give yourself at least three hours to write a letter using loving speech. While you write the letter, practice looking deeply into the nature of your relationship. Why has communication been difficult? Why has happiness not been possible? You may want to begin like this:

My dear son,

I know you have suffered a lot during the past many years. I have not been able to help you—in fact, I have made the situation worse. It is not my intention to make you suffer, my son. Maybe I am not skillful enough. Maybe I try to impose my ideas on you, and I make you suffer. In the past I thought you made me suffer—that my suffering was caused by you. Now I realize that I have been responsible for my own suffering, and I have made you suffer. As a father I don't want you to suffer. Please help me. Please tell me of my unskillfulness in the past so that I will not continue to make you suffer, because if you suffer I will suffer too. I need your help, my dear son. We should be a happy couple, father and son. I am determined to do it. Please tell me what is in your heart. I promise to do my best to refrain from saying things or doing things that make you suffer. You need to help me, otherwise it is not possible for me to do it. I can't do it alone. In the past, every time I suffered I was inclined to punish you, and say or do things that made you suffer. I thought that was the way to get relief, but I was wrong. I realize now that anything I say or do that makes you suffer, makes me suffer also. I am determined not to do it anymore. Please help me.

You will find that the person who finishes writing the letter is not the same person who began it. Peace, understanding, and compassion have transformed you. A miracle can be achieved in twenty-four hours. That is the practice of loving speech.

EXTENDED PRACTICES

SOLITUDE

The Buddha was surrounded by thousands of monks. He walked, he sat, he ate among the monks and the nuns, but he always dwelled in his silence. There is a Buddhist text called Sutra on Knowing the Better Way of Living Alone. Living alone does not mean that there's no one around us. Living alone means that we are established firmly in the here and the now, and we are aware of everything that is happening in the present moment. You use your mindfulness to become aware of every feeling, of every perception in yourself and of what is happening around you; and you are always with yourself, you don't lose yourself. That is the ideal way of living a life of solitude. That is the Buddha's definition of the ideal practice of solitude: not to be caught in the past, not to be carried away by the future or by the crowd, but to always be there, body and mind united, becoming aware of what is happening in the present moment.

Without the capacity for being alone, we become poorer and poorer. We don't have enough nourishment for ourselves, and we don't have much to offer others. Learning to live in solitude is very important. Each day we should devote some time to being physically alone, because then it's easier to practice nourishing ourselves and looking deeply.

Solitude is not about being alone high up in the mountains, or in a hut deep in the forest. It's not about hiding ourselves away from civilization. Real solitude comes from a stable heart that does not get carried away by the crowd or our sorrows about the past, our worries about the future or our excitement about the present. We do not lose ourselves; we do not lose our mindfulness. To take refuge in our mindful breathing, to come back to the present moment, is to take refuge in the beautiful, serene island within each of us.

That doesn't mean it's impossible to practice being alone and looking deeply when we're with a crowd of people. It is possible. Even if we're in a marketplace, we can be alone and not be carried away by the crowd. We are still ourselves. We are still ourselves even if we are in a group discussion and there is collective emotion. We still dwell safely and solidly in our own island.

Practice

The first step is to be physically alone. The second step is to be yourself and to live in solitude, even when in a group. Living in solitude doesn't mean you cut yourself off from others. It's because you're in solitude that you can be in communion with the world. I feel connected to you because I am fully myself. It's so simple. To really relate to the world, you have to first go back and relate to yourself.

Practice sitting meditation, walking, meals, and working with others, but always come back to your own island as well. Enjoy being together with your family and friends without getting caught and lost in the group emotions and perceptions. Your community, your Sangha, is your support. When you see someone in your community acting in mindfulness, speaking with love, and enjoying her work, she is your reminder to return to your own source of mindfulness, and return to solitude.

When you enjoy your time with the people and friends around you and you don't feel lost in your interactions with others, then even in the midst of society, you can smile and breathe in peace, dwelling in the island of self.

SILENCE

Silence is something that comes from our own hearts, and not from someone outside. If we are truly silent, then no matter what situation we find ourselves in, we can enjoy the silence. Silence does not only mean not talking and not doing loud things. Silence means that we're not disturbed inside; there's no talking inside. There are moments when we think that we are silent and that all around is silent, but there's talking going on all the time inside our head. That's not silence.

The practice is not creating silence outside of our activities, but creating silence within them. Eating with others in a Sangha or family is an opportunity to enjoy silence. Sitting and walking meditation are opportunities for silence, as is listening to a Dharma talk, a Buddhist teacher talking about the Buddha's teachings. When we are silent inside, awareness can penetrate into the soil of our souls.

Practice

At retreats in the Plum Village practice centers, a period of deep silence is observed starting from the end of the evening sitting meditation until after breakfast the next morning. Allow the silence and the calmness to penetrate your flesh and bones. Allow the energy of the Sangha and its mindfulness to penetrate your body and mind. Return to your sleeping space slowly, aware of every step. Breathe deeply and enjoy the stillness and the freshness. Even if there is a person walking by your side, maintain your silence; this person needs your support too. You can stay alone outside with the trees and the stars, then go inside, use the bathroom, change your clothes, and go to bed right away.

Lying on your back, you can practice Deep Relaxation until sleep comes. In the morning, move mindfully and silently to the bath-room, taking time to breathe, and then proceed right away to the meditation hall. You do not have to wait for anyone. When you see someone along the path, just join your palms and bow, allowing him to enjoy the morning the way you do.

LAZY DAY

Many of us are overscheduled, even our children are overscheduled. We think keeping busy will satisfy us, but our constant busyness is one of the reasons we suffer from stress and depression. We have pushed ourselves to work too hard and we have pushed our children to work too hard. This is not a civilization. We have to change the situation.

A Lazy Day is a day for us to be without any scheduled activities. We just let the day unfold naturally, timelessly. We may do walking meditation on our own or with a friend or do sitting meditation in the forest. We might like to read lightly or write home to our family or to a friend.

It can be a day for us to look more deeply at our practice and at our relations with others. We may learn a lot about how we have been practicing. We may recognize what to do or not to do in order to bring more harmony into our practice. Sometimes, we may force ourselves too much in the practice, creating disharmony within and around us. On this day, we have a chance to balance ourselves. We may recognize that we may simply need to rest or that we should practice more diligently. It is a very quiet day for everyone.

When we do not have something to do, we get bored and seek for something to do or for entertainment. We are very afraid of being there and doing nothing. The Lazy Day has been prescribed for us to train ourselves not to be afraid of doing nothing. Otherwise, we have no means to confront our stress and depression. It is only when we get bored and become aware that we are seeking entertainment to hide the feelings of loneliness and worthlessness in ourselves that the tension, the depression, the stress begin to dissolve. We can arrange our daily lives so we have opportunities to learn being peace, being joy, being loving, and being compassionate.

Practice

A Lazy Day isn't a day when you can just do what you like. On most days you have so many things to do for other people, daily things, and there are things you would very much like to do for yourself. But that is not the Lazy Day. Lazy Day is a day when you refrain from doing anything. You resist doing things. Because you are used to always doing something, it has become a bad habit. The Lazy Day is a kind of drastic measure against that kind of habit energy.

On Lazy Days, you do your best to refrain from doing something. Try to do nothing. It's hard. It's hard, but you can learn a new way of being. You think that when you're not doing anything, you're wasting your time. That's not true. Your time is, first of all, for you to be: to be alive, to be peace, to be joy, and to be loving. The world needs joyous and loving people who are capable of just being without doing. If you know the art of being peace, of being solid, then you have the ground for every action. The ground for action is to be, and the quality of being determines the quality of doing. And action must be based on non-action. We usually say: "Don't just sit there, do something." But we have to reverse that statement to say: "Don't just do something, sit there," in order to be in such a way that peace, understanding, and compassion are possible.

LISTENING TO A DHARMA TALK

The teachings of the Buddha are called the Dharma. If you attend a retreat at a practice center, or if you go to a sitting group or class in your neighborhood that is led by a lay Dharma teacher, you will have the opportunity to hear a Dharma talk.

Practice

Arrive early for the talk so that you may have enough time to find a seat and establish yourself in a peaceful state of mind. Listen to the talks with an open mind and a receptive heart. If you listen only with your intellect, comparing and judging what is said to what you already think you know or what you have heard others say, you may miss the chance to truly receive the message that is being transmitted.

The Dharma is like rain. Let it penetrate deeply into your consciousness, watering the seeds of wisdom and compassion that are already there. Absorb the talk openly, like the earth receiving a refreshing spring rain. The talk might be just the condition our tree needs to flower and bear the fruits of understanding and love.

Out of respect for the teachings and the teacher, you are asked to sit on a chair or a cushion during the teachings and not to lie down. If you feel tired during the talk, mindfully shift your position and practice deep breathing and gentle massage for one or two minutes to bring fresh oxygen to your brain and the areas of fatigue in your body.

Refrain from talking or making disturbing noises during the Dharma talk. If it is absolutely necessary to leave during the talk, please do so with a minimum of disturbance to others.

DHARMA DISCUSSION

Dharma discussion is an opportunity to benefit from each other's insights and experience of the practice. It is a special time for us to share our experiences, our joys, our difficulties, and our questions relating to the practice of mindfulness. By practicing deep listening while others are speaking, we help create a calm and receptive environment. By learning to speak out about our happiness and our difficulties in the practice, we contribute to the collective insight and understanding of the group.

Practice

Base your sharing only on your own experience of the practice rather than about abstract ideas and theoretical topics. Many of us share similar difficulties and aspirations. Sitting, listening, and sharing together, you recognize your true connections to others. One person shares at a time. While that person is speaking, everyone follows their breathing and listens deeply without judging or reacting, and without making cross talk or offering advice.

Remember that whatever is shared during the Dharma discussion time is confidential. If a friend shares about a difficulty she is facing, respect that she may or may not wish to talk about this outside of the Dharma discussion time.

Discussing the Dharma in the ultimate dimension,
we look at each other and smile.
You are me, don't you see?
Speaking and listening, we are one.

TOUCHING THE EARTH

The practice of Touching the Earth, also known as bowing deeply or prostrating, helps us return to the earth and to our roots, and to recognize that we are not alone but connected to a whole stream of spiritual and blood ancestors. We touch the earth to let go of the idea that we are separate and to remind us that we are the earth and part of life.

When we touch the earth we become small, with the humility and simplicity of a young child. When we touch the earth we become great, like an ancient tree sending her roots deep into the earth, drinking from the source of all waters. When we touch the earth, we breathe in all the strength and stability of the earth, and breathe out our suffering—our feelings of anger, hatred, fear, inadequacy, and grief.

Practice

To begin this practice, join your palms in front of your chest in the shape of a lotus bud. Then gently lower yourself to the ground so that your shins, forearms, and forehead are resting comfortably on the floor. While touching the earth, turn your palms face up, showing your openness to the Three Jewels—the Buddha, Dharma, and Sangha. Breathe in all the strength and stability of the earth, and breathe out to release your clinging to any suffering. After one or two times of practicing Touching the Earth, you can already release a lot of your suffering and feeling of alienation and reconcile with your ancestors, parents, children, or friends.

Touching the Earth is a practice that is helpful to do with your Sangha. When you are with a Sangha, one person can be the bell master and invite the bell between prostrations. This same person can read The Five Earth Touchings aloud while everyone prostrates. If you practice Touching the Earth on your own, you can make a recording of yourself reading the text or do it from memory.

THE FIVE EARTH TOUCHINGS

In gratitude, I bow to all generations of ancestors in my blood family.

I see my mother and father, whose blood, flesh, and vitality are circulating in my own veins and nourishing every cell in me. Through them I see my four grandparents. I carry in me the life, blood, experience, wisdom, happiness, and sorrow of all generations. I open my heart, flesh, and bones to receive the energy of insight, love, and experience transmitted to me by my ancestors. I know that parents always love and support their children and grandchildren, although they are not always able to express it skillfully because of difficulties they encounter. As a continuation of my ancestors, I allow their energy to flow through me, and ask for their support, protection, and strength.

In gratitude, I bow to all generations of ancestors in my spiritual family.

I see in myself my teachers, the ones who show me the way of love and understanding, the way to breathe, smile, forgive, and live deeply in the present moment. I open my heart and my body to receive the energy of understanding, loving kindness, and protection from the Awakened Ones, their teachings, and the community of practice over many generations. I vow to practice to transform the suffering in myself and the world, and to transmit their energy to future generations of practitioners.

In gratitude, I bow to this land and all of the ancestors who made it available.

I see that I am whole, protected, and nourished by this land and all of the living beings that have been here and made life worthwhile and possible for me through all their efforts. I see myself touching my ancestors of Native American origin who have lived on this land for such a long time and know the ways to live in peace and harmony with nature, protecting the mountains, forests, animals, vegetation, and minerals of this land. I feel the energy of this land penetrating my body and soul, supporting and accepting me. I vow to contribute my part in transforming the violence, hatred, and delusion that still lie deep in the consciousness of this society so that future generations will have more safety, joy, and peace. I ask this land for its protection and support.

In gratitude and compassion, I bow down and transmit my energy to those I love.

All the energy I have received I now want to transmit to my father, my mother, everyone I love, and all who have suffered and worried because of me and for my sake. I want all of them to be healthy and joyful. I pray that all ancestors in my blood and spiritual families will focus their energies toward each of them, to protect and support them. I am one with those I love.

In understanding and compassion, I bow down to reconcile myself with all those who have made me suffer.

I open my heart and send forth my energy of love and understanding to everyone who has made me suffer, to those who have destroyed much of my life and the lives of those I love. I know now that these people have themselves undergone a lot of suffering and that their hearts are overloaded with pain, anger, and hatred. I pray that they can be transformed to experience the joy of living, so that they will not continue to make themselves and others suffer. I see their suffering and do not want to hold any feelings of hatred or anger in myself toward them. I do not want them to suffer. I channel my energy of love and understanding to them and ask all my ancestors to help them.

TRAVELING AND RETURNING HOME

We are used to traveling a lot. Even when we go on a vacation, or come to a practice center or another place of rest, we are already often planning our day trips or escapes. At Plum Village, we refrain from traveling into town as much as we can. Our time spent here at the practice center is very precious. There are many nurturing elements of peace and happiness here, such as the beautiful trees and forests, the birds, our brothers and sisters who have come from all walks of life to practice like us. The collective energy of the Sangha is the most precious thing. We spend our time devoted to the practice.

Often, once people have found a place where they can relax or have made a home at one of the practice centers, they feel sad when the time comes to leave. But there is no coming and no going, for we are always with you, and you with us. When you go home, remember to return to your breathing. You will know that the friends at Plum Village and our Sangha body all over the world are breathing too.

Practice

On the day that you are traveling or are leaving to go on a trip, invite a bell fifteen minutes before the departure time. Allow your-self enough time for preparation so you won't have to rush. Begin heading toward the bus, car, or van so that you will not be late and keep the others waiting. Walk mindfully and enter a car that has an empty seat. Sit up straight and follow your breathing. You might like to observe the surrounding countryside. Refrain from being carried away by conversations.

Continue your practice as you return to your home, your family, and society. As you have learned to live in harmony with the Sangha in Plum Village, you can also cultivate harmony in your family and in society. As you have learned to understand and appreciate your friends in the practice, you can also learn to understand and appreciate your coworkers and your neighbors. You can practice loving speech with strangers on the city bus, just as you do with the sisters and brothers at Plum Village. Mindfulness practice is everywhere you go.

Anywhere, any time you like, you can take refuge in the practices of conscious breathing, mindful eating, loving speech, deep listening, and many other wonderful practices. When you do, you will feel very connected and not alone. You become as large as the whole community, the whole Sangha body.

METTA/LOVE MEDITATION

To love is, first of all, to accept ourselves as we actually are. That is why in this Love Meditation, "Knowing Thyself" is the first practice of love. When we practice this, we see the conditions that have caused us to be the way we are. This makes it easy for us to accept ourselves, including our suffering and our happiness at the same time.

One day, King Prasenajit of Koshala asked Queen Mallika, "My dear wife, is there anyone who loves you as much as you love your-self?" The queen laughed and responded, "My dear husband, is there anyone who loves you more than you love yourself?" The next day, they told the Buddha of their conversation, and he said, "You are correct. There is no one in the universe more dear to us than our-selves. The mind may travel in a thousand directions, but it will find no one else more beloved. The moment you see how important it is to love yourself, you will stop making others suffer."

Metta means loving kindness. We begin this with an aspiration: "May I be...." Then we transcend the level of aspiration and look deeply at all the positive and negative characteristics of the object of our meditation, in this case, ourselves. The willingness to love is not yet love. We look deeply, with all our being, in order to understand. We don't just repeat the words, or imitate others, or strive after some ideal. The practice of love meditation is not auto-suggestion. We don't just say, "I love myself. I love all beings." We look deeply at our body, our feelings, our perceptions, our mental formations, and our consciousness, and in just a few weeks, our aspiration to love will become a deep intention. Love will enter our thoughts, our words, and our actions, and we will notice that we have become peaceful, happy, and light in body and spirit; safe and free from injury; and free from anger, afflictions, fear, and anxiety.

When we practice, we observe how much peace, happiness, and lightness we already have. We notice whether we are anxious about accidents or misfortunes, and how much anger, irritation, fear, anxiety, or worry are already in us. As we become aware of the feelings in us, our self-understanding will deepen. We will see how our fears and lack of peace contribute to our unhappiness, and we will see the value of loving ourselves and cultivating a heart of compassion.

In this love meditation, "anger, afflictions, fear, and anxiety" refer to all the unwholesome, negative states of mind that dwell in us and rob us of our peace and happiness. Anger, fear, anxiety, craving, greed, and ignorance are the great afflictions of our time. By practicing mindful living, we are able to deal with them, and our love is translated into effective action.

Practice

This is a love meditation adapted from the Visuddhimagga (The Path of Purification) by Buddhaghosa, a fifth-century C.E. systematization of the Buddha's teachings.

To practice this love meditation, sit still, calm your body and your breathing, and recite it to yourself. The sitting position is a wonderful position for practicing this. Sitting still, you are not too preoccupied with other matters, so you can look deeply at yourself as you are, cultivate your love for yourself, and determine the best ways to express this love in the world.

> *May I be peaceful, happy, and light in body and spirit.*
> *May she be peaceful, happy, and light in body and spirit.*
> *May he be peaceful, happy, and light in body and spirit.*
> *May they be peaceful, happy, and light in body and spirit.*
>
> *May I be safe and free from injury.*
> *May she be safe and free from injury.*
> *May he be safe and free from injury.*
> *May they be safe and free from injury.*
>
> *May I be free from anger, afflictions, fear, and anxiety.*

*May she be free from anger,
afflictions, fear, and anxiety.
May he be free from anger,
afflictions, fear, and anxiety.
May they be free from anger,
afflictions, fear, and anxiety.*

Begin practicing this love meditation on yourself ("I"). Until you are able to love and take care of yourself, you cannot be of much help to others. After that, practice on others ("he/she," "they")—first on someone you like, then on someone neutral to you, then on someone you love, and finally on someone the mere thought of whom makes you suffer.

According to the Buddha, a human being is made of five elements, called *skandhas* in Sanskrit. These skandhas are form, feelings, perceptions, mental formations, and consciousness. In a way, you are the surveyor, and these elements are your territory. To know the real situation within yourself, you have to know your own territory, including the elements within you that are at war with each other. In order to bring about harmony, reconciliation, and healing within, you have to understand yourself. Looking and listening deeply, surveying your territory, is the beginning of love meditation.

Begin this practice by looking deeply into the skandha of form, that is, your body. Ask: How is my body in this moment? How was it in the past? How will it be in the future? Later, when you meditate on someone you like, someone neutral to you, someone you love, and someone you hate, you also begin by looking at his physical aspects. Breathing in and out, visualize his face; his way of walking, sitting, and talking; his heart, lungs, kidneys, and all the organs in his body, taking as much time as you need to bring these details into awareness. But always start with yourself. When you see your own five skandhas clearly, understanding and love arise naturally, and you know what to do and what not to do.

Look into your body to see whether it is at peace or suffering from illness. Look at the condition of your lungs, your heart, your intestines, your kidneys, and your liver to see what the real needs of your body are. When you do, you will eat, drink, and act in ways that demonstrate your love and your compassion for your body. Usually you follow ingrained habits. But when you look deeply, you see that many of these habits harm your body and mind, so you work to transform your habits in ways conducive to good health and vitality.

Next, observe your feelings—whether they are pleasant, unpleasant, or neutral. Feelings flow in us like a river, and each feeling is a drop of water in that river. Look into the river of your feelings and see how each feeling came to be. See what has been preventing you from being happy, and do your best to transform those things. Practice touching the wondrous, refreshing, and healing elements that are already in you and in the world. Doing so, you become stronger and better able to love yourself and others.

Then meditate on your perceptions. The Buddha observed, "The person who suffers most in this world is the person who has many wrong perceptions, and most of our perceptions are erroneous." You see a snake in the dark and you panic, but when your friend shines a light on it, you see that it is only a rope. You have to know which wrong perceptions cause us to suffer. Please write beautifully the sentence, "Are you sure?" on a piece of paper and tape it to your wall. Love meditation helps you learn to look with clarity and serenity in order to improve the way you perceive.

Next, observe your mental formations, the ideas and tendencies within you that lead you to speak and act as you do. Practice looking deeply to discover the true nature of your mental formations—how you are influenced by your individual consciousness and also by the collective consciousness of your family, ancestors, and society. Unwholesome mental formations cause so much disturbance; wholesome mental formations bring about love, happiness, and liberation.

Finally, look at your consciousness. According to Buddhism, consciousness is like a field with every possible kind of seed in it: seeds of love, compassion, joy, and equanimity; seeds of anger, fear, and anxiety; and seeds of mindfulness. Consciousness is the storehouse that contains all these seeds, all the possibilities of what might arise in your mind. When your mind is not at peace, it may be because of the desires and feelings in your store consciousness. To live in peace, you have to be aware of your tendencies—your habit energies—so you can exercise some self-control. This is the practice of preventive health care. Look deeply into the nature of your feelings to find their roots, to see which feelings need to be transformed, and nourish those feelings that bring about peace, joy, and well-being.

UNILATERAL DISARMAMENT

What can we do when we're aware we've done something that causes others to be unhappy? The people we make suffer may still be alive. The people we have made suffer may have already died. What can we do to make amends? The wound is not only in the body, in the soul, in the consciousness of the other person, but the wound is there in ourselves. Suppose we said something unkind to our grandmother fifty years ago. The pain, the suffering is still there in our consciousness, in our soul. I know that my grandmother is alive in me with her wound. I am alive also with that same kind of wound. Practicing unilateral disarmament means we disarm ourselves, regardless of what the other person does and regardless of whether the other person is alive or not.

We don't need the other person to be there in order to heal our-selves. We don't need them to sit in front of us in order for us to be reconciled with them. Reconciliation and healing can be realized within oneself alone. And disarmament can be done unilaterally. If we disarm ourselves, if we become peaceful, if we decide not to attack and not to argue, we already have peace inside us. When even one person practices unilateral disarmament, it will already have an effect on the other person.

Practice

When you are aware of a wound, begin to breathe in and out and begin to be aware of the wound. For example: Breathing in, I am aware of the wound in me; breathing out, I am taking good care of it. Breathing in, I say "I'm sorry, Grandma"; breathing out, "I know I will not do it again."

When you practice like that, you make your grandmother in you smile, and the healing begins to take place. The moment you disarm yourself, the moment you decide to give up the fight, the moment you practice beginning anew in yourself, the healing begins and you undergo a transformation that will very soon have an effect on the other person. She will see the difference in you. And now you are looking at her in a different way, you are smiling at her in a very different way. You are now a flower and no longer a thorn for her. Very soon, she will notice this, and it will be her turn to disarm and transform.

Peace begins with me. Reconciliation begins with me. Healing begins with me. So when you practice deep breathing and smiling to the pain in you, and vow to begin anew, when you practice loving kindness, taking care of your pain and suffering, you are already practicing taking care of the other person. Taking care of yourself is to take care of the other person.

For example, suppose you write a letter of reconciliation after ten years of separation from someone. If your letter is sincere, you will begin to feel much better right away, just during the time of writing. You haven't yet put the letter into the envelope, you haven't put the stamp on, you haven't sent it to the post office, the other person has not yet received it, but you feel very good right now, you have reconciled already with yourself, and your health begins to improve right away. That person would need three or five days to receive the letter and telephone you to thank you, but that is only one of the effects, not the only one.

TALKING TO YOUR INNER CHILD

Many of us have a wounded child within us. We have been deeply wounded as children, making it hard for us to trust and love, and to allow love from others to reach us. Making time to go back to this wounded child is a very important practice. But there can be an obstacle. Many of us know that we have a wounded child within us, but we are afraid to go back to ourselves and be with that child. The block of pain and sorrow in us is so huge and overwhelming that we run away from it. But we need to go home and take care of our wounded child, even though this is difficult. We need instructions on how to do this so that the pain inside does not overwhelm us.

Practice

The practices of mindful walking, mindful sitting, and mindful breathing are crucial. Also, your friends' energy of mindfulness can help. The first time you go home to the wounded child, you may need one or two friends—especially those who have been successful in the practice—sitting next to you, to lend their support, mindfulness, and energy. When a friend sits close to you and holds your hand, you combine his or her energy with your own and so may feel safer to go home and embrace your wounded child within.

When you sit or walk mindfully, talk to your wounded child within, embrace that child with the energy of mindfulness. You can say: "Darling, I am here for you. I will take good care of you. I know that you suffer so much. I have been so busy and neglectful of you, and now I have learned a way to come back to you."

You have to talk to your child several times a day. Only then can healing take place. The little child has been left alone for so long. That is why you have to begin the practice right away. Embracing your child tenderly, you reassure him that you will never let him down again or leave him unattended. If you have a loving

Sangha, then your practice will be easier. To practice alone, without the support of brothers and sisters, is more difficult. Taking refuge in the Sangha and having brothers and sisters to assist you, give advice, and support you in difficult moments is very important.

Your wounded child may represent several generations. Maybe your parents and grandparents had the same problem; they also had a wounded child within that they didn't know how to handle, so they transmitted their wounded child to you. Our practice is to end this vicious cycle. If you can heal your wounded child, you will liberate the person who abused you. That person may also have been the victim of abuse. If you generate the energy of mindfulness, understanding, and compassion for your wounded child, you will suffer much less. People suffer because they have not been touched by compassion and understanding. When you generate mindfulness, compassion and understanding become possible. Then you can allow people to love you. Before, you were suspicious of everything and everyone. Compassion helps you relate to others and restore communication.

THE FOURTEEN MINDFULNESS TRAININGS

The Fourteen Mindfulness Trainings of the Order of Interbeing are a modern version of the fifty-eight bodhisattva precepts set out in the Brahmajala Sutra (Sutra of the Net of Indra).[5] The Fourteen Mindfulness Trainings are mindfulness in our real lives and not just the teaching of ideas. If we practice these trainings deeply, we will recognize that each of them contains all the others. Studying and practicing the mindfulness trainings can help us understand the true nature of interbeing—we cannot just be by ourselves alone; we can only inter-be

---

[5] The Order of Interbeing was founded in 1966, during the war in Vietnam. It has both monastic and lay members. For more information, see Thich Nhat Hanh, Interbeing (Berkeley, CA: Parallax Press, 1998).

with everyone and everything else. To practice these trainings is to become aware of what is going on in our bodies, our minds, and the world. With awareness, we can live our lives happily, fully present in each moment we are alive, intelligently seeking solutions to the problems we face, and working for peace in small and large ways.

When we practice The Five Mindfulness Trainings deeply (described in the Daily Practice section), we are already practicing the Fourteen. If we want to formally receive The Fourteen Mindfulness Trainings and enter the core community of the Order of Interbeing, it is because we wish to become a community leader, to organize the practice in a Sangha. Only when we have the feeling that we have enough time, energy, and interest to take care of a community should we ask for formal ordination. Then we will be working together with other brothers and sisters. Otherwise, The Five Mindfulness Trainings are enough. We can practice The Fourteen Mindfulness Trainings without a formal ceremony, without being ordained as a member of the Order. We can also modify a few words if we like, so it applies to our own tradition.

Practice

THE FIRST MINDFULNESS TRAINING: OPENNESS Aware of the suffering created by fanaticism and intolerance, we are determined not to be idolatrous about or bound to any doctrine, theory, or ideology, even Buddhist ones. Buddhist teachings are guiding means to help us learn to look deeply and to develop our understanding and compassion. They are not doctrines to fight, kill, or die for.

THE SECOND MINDFULNESS TRAINING: NONATTACHMENT TO VIEWS Aware of the suffering created by attachment to views and wrong perceptions, we are determined to avoid being narrow-minded and bound to present views. We shall learn and practice nonattachment from views in order to be open to others' insights and experiences. We are aware that the knowledge we presently possess is not changeless, absolute truth. Truth is found in life, and we will observe life within and around us in every moment, ready to learn throughout our lives.

THE THIRD MINDFULNESS TRAINING: FREEDOM OF THOUGHT Aware of the suffering brought about when we impose our views on others, we are committed not to force others, even our children, by any means whatsoever—such as authority, threat, money, propaganda, or indoctrination—to adopt our views. We will respect the right of others to be different and to choose what to believe and how to decide. We will, however, help others renounce fanaticism and narrowness through compassionate dialogue.

THE FOURTH MINDFULNESS TRAINING: AWARENESS OF SUFFERING Aware that looking deeply at the nature of suffering can help us develop compassion and find ways out of suffering, we are determined not to avoid or close our eyes before suffering. We are committed to finding ways, including personal contact, images, and sounds, to be with those who suffer, so we can understand their situation deeply and help them transform their suffering into compassion, peace, and joy.

THE FIFTH MINDFULNESS TRAINING: SIMPLE, HEALTHY LIVING Aware that true happiness is rooted in peace, solidity, freedom, and compassion, and not in wealth or fame, we are determined not to take as the aim of our life fame, profit, wealth, or sensual pleasure, nor to accumulate wealth while millions are hungry and dying. We are committed to living simply and sharing our time, energy, and material resources with those in need. We will practice mindful consuming, not using alcohol, drugs, or any other products that bring toxins into our own and the collective body and consciousness.

THE SIXTH MINDFULNESS TRAINING: DEALING WITH ANGER Aware that anger blocks communication and creates suffering, we are determined to take care of the energy of anger when it arises and to recognize and transform the seeds of anger that lie deep in our consciousness. When anger comes up, we are determined not to do or say anything, but to practice mindful breathing or mindful walking and acknowledge, embrace, and look deeply into our anger. We will learn to look with the eyes of compassion at those we think are the cause of our anger.

THE SEVENTH MINDFULNESS TRAINING: DWELLING HAPPILY IN THE PRESENT MOMENT Aware that life is available only in the present moment and that it is possible to live happily in the here and now, we are committed to training ourselves to live deeply each moment of daily life. We will try not to lose ourselves in dispersion or be carried away by regrets about the past, worries about the future, or craving, anger, or jealousy in the present. We will practice mindful breathing to come back to what is happening in the present moment. We are determined to learn the art of mindful living by touching the wondrous, refreshing, and healing elements that are inside and around us, and by nourishing seeds of joy, peace, love, and understanding in ourselves, thus facilitating the work of transformation and healing in our consciousness.

THE EIGHTH MINDFULNESS TRAINING: COMMUNITY AND COMMUNICATION Aware that lack of communication always brings separation and suffering, we are committed to training ourselves in the practice of compassionate listening and loving speech. We will learn to listen deeply without judging or reacting and refrain from uttering words that can create discord or cause the community to break. We will make every effort to keep communications open and to reconcile and resolve all conflicts, however small.

THE NINTH MINDFULNESS TRAINING: TRUTHFUL AND LOVING SPEECH Aware that words can create suffering or happiness, we are committed to learning to speak truthfully and constructively, using only words that inspire hope and confidence. We are determined not to say untruthful things for the sake of personal interest or to impress people, nor to utter words that might cause division or hatred. We will not spread news that we do not know to be certain nor criticize or condemn things of which we are not sure. We will do our best to speak out about situations of injustice, even when doing so may threaten our safety.

THE TENTH MINDFULNESS TRAINING: PROTECTING THE SANGHA Aware that the essence and aim of a Sangha is the practice of understanding and compassion, we are determined not to use the Buddhist community for personal gain or profit or transform our community into a political instrument. A spiritual community should, however, take a clear stand against oppression and injustice and should strive to change the situation without engaging in partisan conflicts.

THE ELEVENTH MINDFULNESS TRAINING: RIGHT LIVELIHOOD Aware that great violence and injustice have been done to our environment and society, we are committed not to live with a vocation that is harmful to humans and nature. We will do our best to select a livelihood that helps realize our ideal of understanding and compassion. Aware of global economic, political, and social realities, we will behave responsibly as consumers and as citizens, not investing in companies that deprive others of their chance to live.

THE TWELFTH MINDFULNESS TRAINING: REVERENCE FOR LIFE Aware that much suffering is caused by war and conflict, we are determined to cultivate nonviolence, understanding, and compassion in our daily lives, to promote peace education, mindful mediation, and reconciliation within families, communities, nations, and in the world. We are determined not to kill and not to let others kill. We will diligently practice deep looking with our Sangha to discover better ways to protect life and prevent war.

THE THIRTEENTH MINDFULNESS TRAINING: GENEROSITY Aware of the suffering caused by exploitation, social injustice, stealing, and oppression, we are committed to cultivating loving kindness and learning ways to work for the well-being of people, animals, plants, and minerals. We will practice generosity by sharing our time, energy, and material resources with those who are in need. We are determined not to steal and not to possess anything that should belong to others. We will respect the property of others, but will try to prevent others from profiting from human suffering or the suffering of other beings.

THE FOURTEENTH MINDFULNESS TRAINING: RIGHT CONDUCT (FOR LAYPEOPLE) Aware that sexual relations motivated by craving cannot dissipate the feeling of loneliness but will create more suffering, frustration, and isolation, we are determined not to engage in sexual relations without mutual understanding, love, and a long-term commitment. In sexual relations, we must be aware of future suffering that may be caused. We know that to preserve the happiness of ourselves and others, we must respect the rights and commitments of ourselves and others. We will do everything in our power to protect children from sexual abuse and to protect couples and families from being broken by sexual misconduct. We will treat our bodies with respect and preserve our vital energies (sexual, breath, spirit) for the realization of our bodhisattva ideal. We will be fully aware of the responsibility of bringing new lives into the world, and will meditate on the world into which we are bringing new beings.

(FOR MONASTICS) Aware that the aspiration of a monk or a nun can only be realized when he or she wholly leaves behind the bonds of worldly love, we are committed to practicing chastity and to helping others protect themselves. We are aware that loneliness and suffering cannot be alleviated by the coming together of two bodies in a sexual relationship, but by the practice of true understanding and compassion. We know that a sexual relationship will destroy our life as a monk or a nun, will prevent us from realizing our ideal of serving living beings, and will harm others. We are determined not to suppress or mistreat our body or to look upon our body as only an instrument, but to learn to handle our body with respect. We are determined to preserve vital energies (sexual, breath, spirit) for the realization of our bodhisattva ideal.

PRACTICING WITH CHILDREN

LISTENING TO YOUR PEOPLE

As adults, we may have the feeling we have much wisdom and experience, while children are still young and know very little. So many generations of parents, teachers, and elder brothers and sisters have considered the opinions of children to be unimportant. They feel that children don't have enough experience and that what they think or want doesn't matter. Elders may believe that they know what is best for their younger brothers and sisters. This is not necessarily true. When elders haven't yet fully understood or listened deeply to the difficulties and the deep wishes of their younger brothers and sisters, they can't truly love them. Love has to come from understanding. When love isn't based on understanding, it is harmful. Without being aware of it, parents commonly cause their children to suffer, and elder brothers and sisters cause the younger ones to suffer.

When we force our children to do what we think is best for them, the communication between ourselves and our children breaks down. When there is no more communication between us, how can we be happy? The most important thing is to keep communication alive between parents and children. When the door of communication has been shut, both parents and children suffer. But when we practice good communication, parents and children will share their lives together as friends, and that is the only way to find true happiness.

In a family, we can have a weekly meeting. Sitting together like this we have an opportunity to discuss issues that are important for our happiness. If a child has a difficulty in school or the grown-ups have a dilemma in the workplace, this can be presented and the whole family can offer their insight as to how to improve the situation. The family that practices like this is really like a Sangha, and a Sangha is just like a family, so it is natural if they function in similar ways. We don't have to call ourselves Buddhist to apply these practices in our life. They are simply a matter of bringing peace and joy to our family and our community.

Practice

Loving speech and deep listening are two wonderful methods to open the door of communication with children. As parents, you should not use the language of authority but the language of love when speaking to your children. When you can speak with the language of love and understanding, your children will come to you and tell you their difficulties, suffering, and anxieties. With this kind of communication, you will gain more understanding of your children and be able to love them more. If your love isn't based on understanding, your children won't feel it as love.

To truly love, you can say to your child: "My love, do you think that I understand you well enough? Do you think that I understand your difficulties and your suffering? Please tell me. I want to know so that I can love you in such a way that doesn't hurt you." You can say, "Darling, please tell me the truth. Do you think that I understand you? Do I understand your suffering, your difficulties, and your deepest wishes? If I don't yet understand, then please help me to understand. Because if I don't understand, I'll continue to make you suffer in the name of love." This is what we call loving speech.

When your child is talking, please practice listening deeply. Sometimes your child will say something that surprises you. It may be the opposite of the way you see things. All the same, listen deeply. Please allow your child to speak freely. Do not cut her off as she is talking or criticize what she says. When you listen deeply with all your heart—for half an hour, one hour, or even three hours—you will begin to see her more deeply and understand her more.

Although your child is still very small, he has deep insights and his own special needs. You may begin to realize that for a long time you may have been making your child suffer. If he is suffering, then you will suffer too.

WALKING MEDITATION WITH CHILDREN

Walking with children is a wonderful way to practice mindfulness. You may like to take a child's hand as you walk. He will receive your concentration and stability, and you will receive his freshness and innocence. From time to time, he may want to run ahead and then wait for you to catch up. A child is a bell of mindfulness, reminding us how wonderful life is.

We can remind children that walking meditation is a wonderful way for them to calm down when they have strong feelings or are upset. We can walk with them, reminding them to pay attention to each step.

Practice

At Plum Village, I teach the young people a simple verse to practice while walking. They say, *"Oui, oui, oui,"* as they breathe in, and *"Merci, merci, merci,"* as they breathe out. "Yes, yes, yes. Thanks, thanks, thanks." I want them to respond to life, to society, and to the Earth in a positive way. They enjoy it very much.

I explain walking meditation to them like this, "Just allow yourself to be! Allow yourself to enjoy being in the present moment. The Earth is so beautiful. Enjoy the planet Earth. You are beautiful too, you are a marvel like the Earth."

"Remember that while you are walking, you are not going anywhere, yet every step helps you to arrive. To arrive where? To arrive in the present moment—to arrive in the here and now. You don't need anything else to be happy."

When children walk with this awareness, they are practicing walking meditation.

HELPING CHILDREN WITH ANGER AND OTHER STRONG EMOTIONS

Emotion is only a storm. It comes and it stays for awhile, and then it goes. Children are fully in the center of the storm when it comes. As adults, we can recognize our storm of emotions, smile at it, embrace it, and learn a lot from it. When we are with a child experiencing strong emotions, we need to practice mindful breathing with strong concentration and share this method with the child.

Practice

Every time a child is experiencing a strong emotion, you can hold the child in your arms or just hold their hand and invite them to practice with you. Share with the child your capacity of solidity. "Hold my hand, we'll breathe together, okay?"

Breathing in, I feel my belly expand.
Breathing out, I see my belly contract.
Expand.
Contract.

Breathe together very deeply. Breathe together very slowly. There's no problem. You are passing on your capacity of solidity to the child. The child breathing in feels strong. The child breathing out feels light. Breathing in, the child's mind starts to be calm. Breathing out, the child's mouth can have a little smile.

Some older children and children who get angry more often may like to practice carrying a pebble with them. Then they can go sit near the Buddha, if there is one in your house, or outside under a special tree, on a special rock, or in their room. You can teach them to hold the pebble and say:

Dear Buddha,

Here is my pebble. I am going to practice with it when things go wrong in my day. Whenever I am angry or upset, I will take the pebble in my hand and breathe deeply. I will do this until I calm down.

Encourage them to keep the pebble with them, then when something happens during the day that makes them unhappy, they can reach in their pocket, take hold of the pebble, breathe deeply, and say:

Breathing in, I know that I am angry.
Breathing out, I am taking good care of my anger.

While they are breathing and saying this, they may still be angry. But they are safe, because they are embracing their anger the way a mother embraces her crying baby. After doing this for a while, their temper will begin to calm down, and they will be able to smile at their anger:

Breathing in, I see anger in me.
Breathing out, I smile at my anger.

When they are able to smile, they can put the pebble back into their pocket for another time. This might be a good time to remind children that when we take care of our anger like this, we are being "mindful." Mindfulness acts just like the rays of the sun; without any effort, the sun shines on everything, and everything changes because of it. When we expose our anger to the light of mindfulness, it will change too, like a flower opening to the sun.

You can teach children how to look after their feelings of fear or anger by showing them how to be aware of the rising and falling of their abdomen as they breathe. When children become afraid or angry, if they have forgotten the exercises you showed them, you only have to gently remind them how to practice.

FAMILY MEALS

A few years ago, I asked some children, "What is the purpose of eating breakfast?" One boy replied, "To get energy for the day." Another said, "The purpose of eating breakfast is to eat breakfast." I think the second child is more correct. The purpose of eating is to eat.

We do our best to eat at least one meal a day with the whole family. Eating a meal together, we cultivate more harmony and love as a family. Someone in the family can recite the contemplations or we can sing them together before eating. We use our talent and our creativity to make it pleasant for everyone.

Practice

Practice silent meditation, breathing in and out three times. Look at one another, recognize each other's presence, and eat silently for the first two minutes. You may like to recite the Food Contemplations for Young People:

THE FIRST CONTEMPLATION This food is the gift of the whole universe: the earth, the sky, the rain, and the sun.

THE SECOND CONTEMPLATION We thank the people who have made this food, especially the farmers, the people at the market, and the cooks.

THE THIRD CONTEMPLATION We only put on our plate as much food as we can eat.

THE FOURTH CONTEMPLATION We want to chew the food slowly so that we can enjoy it.

THE FIFTH CONTEMPLATION This food gives us energy to practice being more loving and understanding.

THE SIXTH CONTEMPLATION We eat this food in order to be healthy and happy, and to love each other as a family.

The practice is easy. To be worthy of the food, you only have to eat it mindfully. If you don't eat it mindfully, you're not kind to the food or to the producers of the food. I like to remind myself to eat in moderation. I know food plays an important role in my well-being. That is why I vow to eat only foods that maintain my health and well-being. Both adults and children can practice in this way.

INVITING THE BELL

It's very wonderful to breathe together. It's important that we can breathe mindfully by ourselves, but when the whole family comes together and breathes in and out it creates a wonderful kind of energy, embracing everyone. Our many hearts become one heart and our many lungs become one set of lungs. If it happens that someone is angry or there is quarreling in the family, that's a good time to invite the bell to sound.

Any member of the family has the right to invite the bell to sound when there's not enough peace in the family. When big brother gets angry, or mother is crying, these are times it's very important that someone in the family comes to the bell and asks the bell to sound, so that everyone in the family can practice mindful breathing in and out three times. If we practice like that even for one week, breathing in and out nine times in the morning and the evening and whenever there's not enough peace in the family, there will be more calm and harmony in the family.

Practice

I have many friends, some very young, who love to practice inviting the bell and listening to the bell. In the morning before they go off to school, they sit down, they invite the bell to sound, and they enjoy breathing in and out. With breakfast, the practice of the bell, and breathing in and out, they can start the day with peace, serenity, and solidity. So instead of wishing the other person "have a good day," you can help them begin the good day with the sound of the bell and breathing in and out. And before you go to sleep, you can sit down together as a family and practice the sounds of the bell and breathing in and out together. That would be very beautiful and peaceful.

The practice for inviting the bell is the same for children as it is for adults. You bow to the bell, you put the bell on your hand, and you practice breathing in, breathing out with the poem before you invite the half sound.

Use this poem to breathe in and out, in and out.

> *Body, speech, and mind in perfect oneness,*
> *I send my heart along with the sound of this bell.*
> *May the hearers awaken from forgetfulness*
> *and transcend the path of anxiety and sorrow.*

Then, you make the half sound of the bell. Now, allow people to have time to prepare themselves, the time of one in-breath and one out-breath. Then, you invite a full sound of the bell. After the full sound, there will be breathing in and out three times with this poem:

> *Listen, listen.*
> *This wonderful sound*
> *brings me back*
> *to my true home.*

Listen very deeply and enjoy. That is the practice of peace. And after this moment, invite another full sound of the bell. Breathe in and out three times slowly. Finally, invite the third and the last full sound. Then breathe again three in-breaths and three out-breaths. And after that, you lower the bell and put it on a cushion.

A young bell master should know that her in-breath and out-breath are shorter than the in-breath and out-breath of the adults. So after inviting the bell to sound, she should enjoy breathing in and out three times and then allow little bit more time for the adults to enjoy fully their three in- and out-breaths. She is very kind if she does this, because listening to the bell is the time to enjoy ourselves, to enjoy peace, to enjoy life. I can sit like this and listen to the bell for one hour or more, and I enjoy it. It's very healing, very nourishing.

PEBBLE MEDITATION

I like to carry some pebbles with me in my pocket. In my pocket there is no credit card, no money, and no cigarettes. There may be a sheet of paper, a little bell, something like that.

These pebbles help remind me that we humans are born as flowers in the garden of humanity. If we don't know how to preserve our freshness, then we suffer and we do not have enough beauty to offer to the people we love.

Practice

Make a little bag and put in the bag four pebbles that you have collected outside. You can all sit in a circle, and one child or person in the family plays the role of bell master. After having invited the bell to sound three times and enjoying breathing in and breathing out, pour the pebbles out of the bag and set them on the ground to your left. With your right hand, pick up one pebble and look at it. The first pebble represents a flower. It also represents your own freshness and flower nature.

Put the pebble on the palm of your left hand, and put the left hand on the right hand to begin your meditation on flower nature:

Breathing in, I see myself as a flower.
Breathing out, I feel fresh.

That is not make-believe, because you are a flower in the garden of humanity. See yourself as a flower. It is very helpful to smile during the practice, because a flower is always smiling. Practice flower/fresh three times. After that, take the pebble and put it down on the ground to your right.

Then take the second pebble and look at it. This pebble represents a mountain. A mountain represents solidity. You are yourself, you are stable, and you are solid. Without solidity, you can't be truly happy. You will be pulled away by provocations, anger, fear, regret, or anxiety. This meditation is best practiced in the sitting position because in the half lotus or lotus position your body feels very stable and solid. Even if someone comes and pushes you, you will not fall. After you place the second pebble in your left hand, begin to meditate on the mountain.

Breathing in, I see myself as a mountain.
Breathing out, I feel solid.

Repeat mountain/solid three times. When you are solid, you are no longer shaky in your body and in your mind.

The third pebble represents still water. From time to time, you see a lake where the water is so still that it reflects exactly what is there. It's so still it can reflect the blue sky, the white clouds, the mountains, the trees. You can aim your camera at the lake and take a picture of the sky and the mountain reflected there just the same. When your mind is calm, it reflects things as they are. You aren't a victim of wrong perceptions. When your mind is disturbed by craving, anger, or jealousy, you perceive things wrongly. Wrong perceptions bring us a lot of anger, fear, violence, and push us to do or to say things that will destroy everything. This practice helps you restore your calm and peace, represented by still water.

Breathing in, I see myself as still water.
Breathing out, I reflect things as they truly are.

Repeat water/reflecting three times. This is not wishful thinking. With mindful breathing, you can bring peace to your breath, body, and feelings.

The fourth pebble represents space and freedom. If you do not have enough space in your heart, it will be very difficult for you to feel happy. If you are arranging flowers, you understand that flowers need space around to radiate their beauty. Each person needs some space as well. If you love someone, one of the most precious things you can offer him is space. And this you cannot buy in the super-market. Visualize the moon sailing in the sky. The moon has a lot of space around it, that is part of its beauty. Many of the disciples of the Buddha described him as a full moon sailing in the empty sky.

> *Breathing in, I see myself as space.*
> *Breathing out, I feel free.*

Repeat space/free three times. Each person needs freedom and space. Offer space to the loved ones in your family as well. Without imposing your ideas or ways on the other person, you can offer them the gift of this pebble meditation. In this way, it is possible for you to help remove the worries, fears, and anger in the heart of each person in your family.

THE BREATHING ROOM

Every house should have a room called the Breathing Room, or at least a corner of a room reserved for this purpose. In this place we can put a low table with a flower, a little bell, and enough cushions for everyone in the family to sit on. When we feel uneasy, sad, or angry, we can go into this room, close the door, sit down, invite a sound of the bell, and practice breathing mindfully. When we have breathed like this for ten or fifteen minutes, we begin to feel better. If we do not practice like this, we can lose our temper. Then we may shout or pick a fight with the other person, creating a huge storm in our family.

On one summer retreat at Plum Village, I asked a young boy, "My child, when your father speaks in anger, do you have any way to help your father?" The child shook his head: "I do not know what to do. I become very scared and try to run away." When children come to Plum Village they can learn about the Breathing Room, so they can help their parents when they become angry. I told the young boy, "You can invite your parents into your Breathing Room to breathe with you."

Practice

A Breathing Room or Breathing Corner is something a family must agree about in advance. When everyone is feeling happy, this is a good occasion to ask family members to sign an agreement with each other. You could say: "Sometimes we are angry, and we say hurtful things to you or to each other. This makes you afraid. Next time this happens, we will go into the Breathing Room and invite the sound of the bell to remind us all to breathe." If you live with just one child, you can still ask them to sign this agreement with you, so that when you are feeling angry, she has something she can do to help both of you.

If, at that particular moment, the child that you take care of is feeling happy, she will be very eager to agree.

As a young child, she is still very fresh. She can use her freshness to help her parents. She can say to either one of her parents: "Follow me into the Breathing Room, and let's breathe together instead of arguing. What do you think?"

If only one parent agrees with her, then when the other says something unkind, she can take the parent that agrees by the hand and say to him: "Let's go into the Breathing Room." When the other parent sees this, it may wake her up.

Once you have gone into the Breathing Room, she has the sound of the bell and the Buddha to protect her. Everyone in the family can sign an agreement that states: "When we hear the sound of the bell in the Breathing Room, it is the sound of the Buddha calling us, and everyone in the house will stop and breathe. No one will continue to shout after that." The whole family can make this commitment to stop and breathe at the sound of the bell. This is called The Agreement on Living Together in Peace and Joy. If you can bring this method of practice home, after about three months you will feel that the atmosphere in the family has become much more pleasant. The wounds in the hearts of the children will be soothed, and gradually they will heal.

THE FOUR MANTRAS

This is the kind of practice I would like everyone to bring home and do every day. A mantra is a magic formula. Every time we pronounce a mantra, we transform the situation right away; we don't have to wait. It is a magic formula we have to recite when the time is appropriate. The condition that makes it effective is our mindfulness and concentration, otherwise it will not work.

Practice

Practicing the Four Mantras is the same for adults and children.

THE FIRST MANTRA "Darling, I am here for you." You don't have to practice it in Sanskrit or Tibetan, practice it in your own language. Why do you practice this mantra? Because when you love someone, you have to offer him or her the best you have. And the best that you can offer your beloved one is your true presence.

THE SECOND MANTRA "Darling, I know you are there, and I am very happy." To love means to acknowledge the presence of the person you love. You have to have the time, if you are too busy, how can you acknowledge his presence? The condition for doing this mantra is that you are there one hundred percent. If you are not, then you cannot recognize the person's presence. When someone loves you, you need that person to recognize that you are there—whether you are young or old.

You can only love when you are there, and in order to be there you have to practice being there, whether by mindful breathing or mindful walking, any kind of practice that will help you really be there as a free person for the person you love. Because you are there, you are mindful, which is why you notice when the person you love suffers. In the moment you recognize his suffering, you have to practice deeply to be there one hundred percent. Go to him and pronounce the third mantra.

THE THIRD MANTRA "Darling, I know you suffer, that's why I am here for you." When you suffer, you want the person you love to be aware of your suffering—that's very human, that's very natural. If the person you love doesn't know that you suffer, or if he ignores your suffering, you suffer much more. So it is a great relief if the person you love is aware that you are suffering. Before they do anything to help, they suffer less already. This is not the practice of children alone, this is the practice of everyone. And this can make a lot of happiness in the house. Try it for a few weeks and you will see; the situation in the home will be transformed dramatically.

THE FOURTH MANTRA "Darling, I suffer, please help." The third mantra is practiced when the person you love suffers. You practice the fourth mantra when you yourself suffer. You believe the person you love the most has caused your suffering; that,s why it is so difficult. When the person you love so much says something or does something that hurts you, you suffer quite a lot. If someone else said or did something, you would not suffer that much. But this is the person you love most in the world, and he just did that to you, he just said that to you. That is why you cannot bear it. You suffer one hundred times more. This is when the fourth mantra has to be practiced. You have to go to that person you love the most, who just hurt you very deeply, you go to him or her with full awareness, with full mindfulness and concentration, and you utter the fourth mantra. This is quite difficult. But if you train yourself, you can do it...

Is it possible to practice the fourth mantra? It seems that you don't want to do it, because you feel you don't need his help. You want help from anyone else, but not him. You want to be independent—"I don't need you!" Your pride is deeply hurt, that is why the fourth mantra is so important. Go to him and, breathing in and out deeply, become yourself one hundred percent and just open your mouth and say with all your concentration that you suffer and you need his help.

In order to be able to practice this, you have to train yourself for some time. You may have a tendency to tell this person that you don't need them.

You can survive on your own, completely independent. But if you know how to look at the situation with wisdom, you will see this is an unwise thing to do. Because when we love each other, we need each other, especially when we suffer. Are you so sure your suffering comes from him? Maybe you are wrong. Maybe he has not done that or said that in order to hurt you. Maybe you have misunderstood, maybe you have a wrong perception.

You have to train yourself now in preparation for the next time you suffer so that in that moment, you'll be able to practice the fourth mantra. Practice walking meditation, practice sitting meditation, practice breathing in and out mindfully to restore yourself. Then go to him and practice the mantra: "Darling, I suffer so much. You are the person I love most in the world. Please help me." Don't let your pride stand between you and him. In true love there is no room for pride. If pride is still there, you know that you have to practice to transform your love into true love.

Children are still young, they have plenty of chances to learn and train themselves for the practice. I am confident that if they are taught and practice right now, it will be very easy for them to practice later on when they suffer because they think the person they love most has done that to them, has said that to them. I don't think that they are going to use the fourth mantra often, but it is a very important mantra. Maybe they have to use it only once or twice a year, but it is extremely important. Have them write it down and keep it somewhere, and every time they suffer very much, encourage them to go and look for that mantra and try to practice it.

THE CAKE IN THE REFRIGERATOR

If we have not yet been able to buy a bell or set up a Breathing Room at our home, we can use a cake. It is a very special cake that is not made of flour and sugar like a sponge cake. We can keep eating it, and it is never finished. It is called The Cake in the Refrigerator.

Practice

There will come a day when your child is sitting in the living room, and she sees that her parents are about to lose their temper with each other. As soon as the atmosphere becomes heavy and unpleasant, she can use the practice of the cake to restore harmony in your family. First of all, she breathes in and out three times to give herself enough courage, and then she looks at her mother and says to her: "Mommy, Mommy." Of course she can do this with her father, a grandparent, or any other adult that takes care of her as well. Her mother will look at her and ask, "What is it, my child?" And she will say, "I remember that we have a cake in the refrigerator." Whether or not there is really a cake in the refrigerator does not matter.

Saying "there is a cake in the refrigerator" really means: "Parents, don't make each other suffer anymore." When they hear these words, her parents will understand. Her mother will look at her and say: "Quite right! Will you go outside and arrange the chairs for a picnic while I go and fetch the cake and the tea." When mother says this, she has already found a way out of the dangerous situation. She can run out on to the porch and wait for her. Her mother now has an opportunity to withdraw from the fight. Before the child spoke up, her mother could not stand up and leave since it would be very impolite, and it might pour more oil onto the flames of the other parent's anger. Now, the mother can go into the kitchen. As she opens the refrigerator to take out the cake and boils the water to make the tea, she can follow her breathing. If there is no real cake in the refrigerator, don't worry, she will find something to substitute for the cake. As she prepares the cake and tea, she can smile the half smile to feel lighter in body and spirit.

While the other parent is sitting alone in the living room, he can begin to practice breathing in mindfulness. Gradually his hot temper will calm down. After the tea and the cake have been placed on the table, he may walk out slowly onto the porch to join the tea party in an atmosphere that is light and full of understanding. If the parent inside is hesitant to come out, then the child can run into the house, take his hand, and coax him out by saying, "Please come and have some tea and cake with me."

ORANGE MEDITATION

There are some people who eat an orange but don't *really* eat it. They eat their sorrow, fear, anger, past, and future. They are not really present with body and mind united. When we eat an orange, we can make the eating into a meditation. We sit in such a way that we feel comfortable, solid, and we look at the orange in such a way that we can see the orange as a miracle. Concentration is very important. We know that when we eat an ice cream, if we turn on television we lose the ice cream; we cannot concentrate on our ice cream. Without mindfulness and concentration, we cannot really enjoy ourselves and the orange.

Practice

Have the child hold the orange in the palm of his hand and look and look at it while breathing in and out, so that the orange becomes a reality. If he is not here, totally present, the orange isn't here either. Ask him to see the orange tree, see the orange blossom, see the sun and the rain passing through, and see the tiny fruit form. And now the fruit has grown into a beautiful orange. So just looking and smiling into the orange he gets in touch with the wonders of life. He sometimes ignores the fact that the orange in the palm of his hand is really a miracle, a wonder of life. There are so many wonders of life inside of him and around him. So when he looks at the orange and smiles to the orange in that way, he really sees the orange in its splendor, in its miraculous nature. And suddenly he himself becomes a miracle, because he is a miracle, he is not something less than a miracle. His presence is a miracle. He is a miracle encountering another miracle.

When he looks at the orange deeply, he will be able to see many wonderful things: the sun shining and the rain falling on the orange tree, the orange blossoms, the tiny fruit appearing on the branch, the color of the fruit changing from green to yellow, and then the full-grown orange. Now ask him to slowly begin to peel it. To smell the wonderful scent of the orange peel. To break off a section of the orange and put it into his mouth. To taste its wonderful juice.

The orange tree has taken three, four, or six months to make such an orange for him. Now the orange is ready, and it says, "I am here for you." But if he is not present, he will not hear it. When he is not looking at the orange in the present moment, then the orange is not present either. Being fully present while eating an orange is a delightful experience.

TREE HUGGING

In my home in Plum Village, I planted three cedar trees. I planted them about thirty years ago, and now they are very big and beautiful, and very refreshing. While I am doing walking meditation, I usually stop in front of one of the trees. I bow to it. It makes me feel happy. I touch the bark with my cheek. I smell the tree. I look up at the beautiful leaves. I feel the strength and freshness of the tree. I breathe in and out deeply. It's very pleasant, and sometimes I stay for a long time, just enjoying the lovely tree.

When we touch a tree, we receive something beautiful and refreshing back. Trees are wonderful! They are also solid, even in a storm. We can learn a lot from trees.

Practice

Have the child find a tree that is especially beautiful to her—perhaps it's an apple tree, an oak tree, or a pine tree. If she stops and touches a tree deeply, she will feel its wonderful qualities. Breathing deeply will help her touch the tree deeply. Have her breathe in, touch the tree, then breathe out. Do this three times. Touching the tree in this way will make her feel refreshed and happy.

Then, if she likes, she can hug the tree. Tree hugging is a wonderful practice. When she hugs a tree, a tree never refuses. She can rely on a tree. It is dependable. Every time she wants to see it, every time she needs its shade, it is there for her.

TODAY'S DAY

We have all sorts of special days. There is a special day to remember fathers. We call it Father's Day. There is a special day to celebrate our mothers. We call it Mother's Day. There is a New Year's Day, Labor Day, and Earth Day. One day a young person visiting Plum Village said, "Why not declare today as Today's Day?" And all the children agreed that we should celebrate today and call it Today's Day.

Practice

On this day, Today's Day, don't think about yesterday, don't think about tomorrow, only think about today. Today's Day is when we live happily in the present moment. When we eat, we know that we are eating. When we drink water, we are aware that it is water we are drinking. When we walk, we really enjoy each step. When we play, we are really present in our play.

Today is a wonderful day. Today is the most wonderful day. That does not mean that yesterday was not wonderful. But yesterday is already gone. It does not mean that tomorrow will not be wonderful. But tomorrow is not yet here. Today is the only day available to us today, and we can take good care of it. That is why today is so important—the most important day of our lives.

So each morning when the child wakes up, have him decide to make that day the most important day. Before he goes off to school, tell him to sit or lie down, breathe slowly in and out for a few minutes, enjoy his in-breath, enjoy his out-breath, and smile. He is here. He is content. He is peaceful. This is a wonderful way to begin a day.

Ask him to try to keep this spirit alive all day; to remember to go back to his breath, to look at other people with loving kindness, to smile and be happy with the gift of life. Have a good day today. This is not only a wish. This is a practice.

CONCLUSION

All these practices have the same basic purpose: to bring our minds back to our bodies, to produce our true presence, and to become fully alive so that everything happens in the light of mindfulness. Each practice in itself is very simple. We breathe in and we breathe out; we make a step in mindfulness; we listen deeply to the ones we love and look closely at the beauty around us. But these simple practices can help us touch our true nature of no birth and no death and no separation.

If we want peace in ourselves and in our world, we have to practice. If we don't practice, we don't have enough of the energy of mindfulness to take care of our fear and anger and the fear and anger of our loved ones. Mindfulness practice is essential for our survival, our peace, and our protection. I hope that at least some of the practices in this book resonate with you. All of us, as well as our families, our society, and our world, need the wisdom and insight that comes from practicing mindfulness and looking deeply.

In Buddhism, there's a wonderful image of the world, full of bright shiny jewels. This world is called the *Dharmakaya*. When we look closely, we can see that the Dharmakaya is our everyday world. We have a rich inheritance, but we don't know it. We behave as if we were poor; a destitute son or daughter. Instead we can recognize that we have a treasure of enlightenment, understanding, love, and joy inside us. It's time to go back to receive our inheritance. These practices can help us claim it.

OUR TRUE HERITAGE

> The cosmos is filled with precious gems.
> I want to offer a handful of them to you this morning.
> Each moment you are alive is a gem,
> shining through and containing earth and sky,
> water and clouds.

It needs you to breathe gently
for the miracles to be displayed.
Suddenly you hear the birds singing,
the pines chanting,
see the flowers blooming,
the blue sky,
the white clouds,
the smile and the marvelous look
of your beloved.

You, the richest person on Earth,
who have been going around
begging for a living,
stop being the destitute child.
Come back and claim your heritage.
We should enjoy our happiness
and offer it to everyone.
Cherish this very moment.
Let go of the stream of distress
and embrace life fully in your arms.

—*Thich Nhat Hanh*

Image I

Parallax Press, a nonprofit organization, publishes books on engaged Buddhism and the practice of mindfulness by Thich Nhat Hanh and other authors. All of Thich Nhat Hanh's work is available at our online store and in our free catalog. For a copy of the catalog, please contact:

Parallax Press
P.O. Box 7355
Berkeley, CA 94707
Tel: (510)525-0101
www.parallax.org

Image II

Monastics and laypeople practice the art of mindful living in the tradition of Thich Nhat Hanh at retreat communities in France and the United States. To reach any of these communities, or for information about individuals and families joining for a practice period, please contact:

Plum Village
13 Martineau
33580 Dieulivol, France
www.plumvillage.org

Blue Cliff Monastery
3 Mindfulness Road
Pine Bush, NY 12566
www.bluecliffmonastery.org

Deer Park Monastery
2499 Melru Lane
Escondido, CA 92026
www.deerparkmonastery.org

The *Mindfulness Bell,* a journal of the art of mindful living in the tradition of Thich Nhat Hanh, is published three times a year by Plum Village. To subscribe or to see the worldwide directory of Sanghas, visit www.mindfulnessbell.org

BACK COVER MATERIAL

Zen Master Thich Nhat Hanh's key teaching is that through mindfulness, we can learn to live in the present moment and develop a sense of peace. Accessible to those new to Buddhist teachings as well as more experienced practitioners, *Happiness* is the only book that collects all practices adapted and developed by Thich Nhat Hanh in his more than 60 years as a Buddhist monk and teacher.

With sections on Daily Practice, Relationships, Physical Practices, Mindful Eating, and Practicing with Children, *Happiness* is a comprehensive guide to living our daily lives with full awareness, whether we are working, eating, parenting, driving, walking, or simply sitting and breathing. Thich Nhat Hanh says, "Enjoy your practice with a relaxed and gentle attitude, with an open mind and receptive heart.... Joy and happiness are available to you in the here and now."

Thich Nhat Hanh is a Vietnamese Buddhist monk whose lifelong efforts to generate peace and reconciliation moved Martin Luther King, Jr. to nominate him for the Nobel Peace Prize in 1967. He lives in southwest France and travels regularly, leading retreats on the art of mindful living. He is the author of *The Energy of Prayer, Being Peace,* and many other best-selling books.

www.ingramcontent.com/pod-product-compliance
Lightning Source LLC
Chambersburg PA
CBHW060558230426
43670CB00011B/1868